Teach Me How to Whisper

Teach Me How to Whisper

"Horses" and Other Poems

Gjekë Marinaj

Translated by Gjekë Marinaj
and Frederick Turner

With an Introduction by Frederick Turner

Syracuse University Press

Copyright © 2023 by Gjekë Marinaj
Syracuse University Press
Syracuse, New York 13244-5290

All Rights Reserved

First Edition 2023

23 24 25 26 27 29   6 5 4 3 2 1

∞ The paper used in this publication meets the minimum requirements
of the American National Standard for Information Sciences—Permanence
of Paper for Printed Library Materials, ANSI Z39.48-1992.

For a listing of books published and distributed by Syracuse University Press,
visit https://press.syr.edu.

ISBN: 978-0-8156-1163-9 (paperback)
    978-0-8156-5698-2 (e-book)

Library of Congress Cataloging-in-Publication Data

Names: Marinaj, Gjekë, 1965– author, translator. | Turner, Frederick,
    1943– translator.
Title: Teach me how to whisper : Horses and other poems / Gjekë Marinaj ;
    translated by Gjekë Marinaj and Frederick Turner.
Description: First edition. | Syracuse : Syracuse University Press, 2023.
Identifiers: LCCN 2023038297 (print) | LCCN 2023038298 (ebook) |
    ISBN 9780815611660 (hardcover) | ISBN 9780815611639 (paperback) |
    ISBN 9780815656982 (ebook)
Subjects: LCSH: Marinaj, Gjekë, 1965—Translations into English. |
    LCGFT: Poetry.
Classification: LCC PG9621.M285 A2 2023 (print) | LCC PG9621.M285
    (ebook) | DDC 891/.9911—dc23/eng/20230914
LC record available at https://lccn.loc.gov/2023038297
LC ebook record available at https://lccn.loc.gov/2023038298

Manufactured in the United States of America

Contents

Introduction
  The Pilot of Hyperbole ix
Self-Portrait xxix

Home
My Neighbors in Brrut 3
My Home in Brrut 5
The Lullaby Singers 6
The First Kisses of Nature 8
On My Mother's Birthday 9
Anthem for My Parents 11
Ode to My Parents 12
A Book Gift from My Parents 13

Albania
The Highlanders of Malësia e Madhe 17

The Return of Skënderbeu 18
Skënderbeu's Advantage 19
Since the Time They Killed Omer 20
The Fortune-Teller 22
Why Do You Look at Me Like That? 23
Bubbles in the Adriatic 24
Lament 26
The Secret of the Immigrants 27
Yesterday 28
Hoping to Find Refuge in America 29
Without Immunity 31
To Shkoder 32
With My Head in the Lap of Kosovo 34
The Balance 36
Riddle 37

Amor
As the Dew Kisses the Mountains, but Sweeter Still *41*
We Were Adolescents and Put off Love until Tomorrow *42*
Where Is the Girl? *43*
Winter *44*
She Makes the Horizon Blush *45*
One World Ocean *47*
Because One Day I Saw You with the Sea *49*
In the Incubator of Grabuta *52*
She Brought Cancun to Its Knees *54*
Your Eyes *55*
Twenty-Four Hours of Love *56*
Dusita *58*
Purgatory
 An Obsolete Ballad *60*
Reading Poetry with My Sweetheart *63*
We Are Born to Love *64*
A Dawn with Two Suns *66*
Evening *67*
A Freudian Moment *68*
In a Curdled Mirror *69*
Another One on COVID-19 *71*
Classi-Five *72*

Admonitions
Horses *77*
Whispering to Hiroshima *78*
The Ambulances of Dallas *80*
The Somali Children *81*
A Foggy Human Dawn *82*
Peace at Zero *83*
Hot Air *84*
The Stranger's Eyes *86*
The Darkangel *87*
Recurring Daymare *88*
The Kronoses of the Twentieth Century *89*
Spit *91*
Sketches in Imagination *92*

Acheron
A Moment of Terror *95*
On the Ferryboat of Acheron *96*
My Conversation with Death *99*

The Death of Jiva
    Novaković *101*
The Poet's Mother Gives
    up the Spirit *102*
Epitaph for a Poet *104*

Heroines
Antigone *109*
The Em Dash of Emily
    Dickinson *110*
Unhappy Brides *111*
Rozafa's Confession *113*
The Desperation of
    Desdemona *114*
Looking into Your Kind
    Eyes *115*
My Mother's Hand *117*
The Highland
    Singer *118*
Mother Teresa *119*
Gonxhe Bojaxhiu *120*

Metaphysics
Truth *123*
Hallelujah *124*
While Seconds Turn to
    Minutes *126*
The Labyrinth of Tang
    Thought *127*
The Spontaneous Energies
    of Matter *128*

A Journey to the Center
    of the Self *129*

Poets
With Neruda on the
    Atlantic Shore *133*
Snow in Beograd *135*
The Poet Frederik Rreshpja
    Was Born Today *137*
The Poet *140*
Sunday Prayer *141*
Where Can I Find the
    Spirit of the Poet? *142*
The Poets Start Over on
    Mondays *143*
Homer *145*
Meadow *146*
To the Birds *147*
The Cave Bear in the Trial
    of Words *149*
Poetry *151*
Prose *152*
Where Was I Last
    Night? *153*
Haiku *154*

Earth
The Blue Nile *157*
Fuji *159*
Sokolovac, Summer
    1998 *160*

So It Seems, at Ha Long
   Bay *162*
Footprints in
   Hollywood *165*
Eiffel Tower *166*
Abstraction *167*

India
To Be a Guest in the House
   of Rita De *171*

The Lost Layers
of Vyasa's Skin
Part 1 *175*
Part 2 *177*
Part 3 *179*
Part 4 *182*
Part 5 *186*
Part 6 *188*
Part 7 *190*
Part 8 *195*
Part 9 *197*
Part 10 *202*
Part 11 *205*
Part 12 *214*
Part 13 *217*
Part 14 *223*

Introduction

The Pilot of Hyperbole

Frederick Turner

At the end of Gjekë Marinaj's visionary mini epic, *The Lost Layers of Vyasa's Skin*, the poet-pilgrim is given a golden egg containing a book of divine-natural wisdom. But he must return it to its guardians, for if it is revealed as explicit knowledge humanity will not be ready for it. What he has learned can only be imparted in the hermetic metaphors of poetry.

What does he mean by "hermetic metaphors"? In his poem "Homer," which could be taken as a definition, he begins with a little joke:

> Homer decoded
> the abstractions
> of the old philosophers—

Marinaj is aware of the Greek and German tradition that holds that all philosophy is a decoding of the great poets (usually Homer and Goethe). Here he paradoxically reverses the idea, making Homer the poet into the great decoder as he interprets the findings of more ancient philosophers who burrowed into the pyramids to discover the "pre-Morse" alphabet, the mind of the Sphinx:

> Those trails they blazed
> in the Sphinx's pyramids
> down to the center of their thought,
>
> the pre-Morse alphabet
> inscribed
> into the songs of Solomon.

A pre-Morse alphabet would presumably be one which is even more primal than the binary Morse code of dots and dashes (or the zeros and ones of the transistor output in a Turing computer). In the poem that alphabet is found inscribed into the intoxicated love songs of King Solomon.[1]

> Pure he kept it,
> far from the antique misconception
> that everything true must be in ink and paper.

But Homer keeps that alphabet pure: these songs are not ink and paper. They are oral codes, which together resemble a bale of wool brought by a shearer to the old spinning ladies in Marinaj's childhood mountain

---

1. A quantum programming language.

village home—or like the body of remembered tales the local *guslers* told that would be spun orally into a coffeehouse performance.

> He redefined the oral codes,
> spun their great bale of wool onto two spindles
> between the letter *I* and the number *0*.

The *I* and the *0* are, of course, the *Iliad* and the *Odyssey*. But they are also the true and false of Aristotelian logic and the one and zero of the computer and the *I* of the ego and the *Oh* of nothingness that confronts it in death. (Marinaj is not above multilingual puns.) Like Clotho, the spinner of the Fates, Marinaj's Homer reduces the cloud of fiber to a narrative line or thread that can form a cloth or fabric. But he knows that those two spindles—the warp and the woof of the weaver—contain the same indeterminate organic substance.

Puzzling out the extended hermetic metaphors is a process that coheres in a larger and stranger insight. *Hermetic* means what belongs to Hermes the god of travelers, the psychopomp between the lands of life and death, identified with the Egyptian god Thoth; he is the master of interpretation whose avatar is Trismegistus, the mythical inventor of writing. Marinaj suggests that Solomon, the first lyric love poet and the patron of the composition of the Talmud, is another version of the same figure. He thus implies that it is a love song, the Song of Solomon, which is at the root of all literacy and all philosophy.

To tease out a few of the poems' rich meanings by paraphrase, as I have done here, is the necessary work of the translator. Even in English Marinaj is so very unlike most poets of today that perhaps a docent would be useful, a "how to read him" guide that can be dismissed at the reader's pleasure, and this is my excuse for not letting the poems immediately speak for themselves. Further, connections that are obvious in Albanian, despite the translator's best efforts to hint at them, may sometimes be lost, and some explanations may help. What is central is Marinaj's large philosophical and moral claims for poetry and his insistence that its means and content are irreplaceable for the world today.

Marinaj's metaphors need to be read as we read Dante Alighieri's sensory allegories, in which physical details, visualized by the reader, add up to an icon, sometimes grotesque, sometimes strangely beautiful, whose meaning is as clear as a piece of logic, but much, much richer. Or as we read John Donne's more elaborate conceits that, silly on the surface, deepen and deepen as they are decoded.

> For poets don't start until the twenty-fifth hour
>   of the day
> When they set out upon the wings of hope
> To thread the rosy tunnel of the afterlife—
> That halfway world where only poets venture:
>
> A world waiting for the gray stars to awaken,
> For it's a place that's lit up only by the poets' sun,

> Where is heard only the chanting bells of the
>   cities of the underworld
> Clanging moist with tears as if reading your
>   poems back to you,
>
> As if they were finishing the farewell speech you
>   never wrote,
> Witnessing the way the last beat of your mitral
>   valve
> Turned to an eye whose lids are the horizons of
>   the world
> That open and close to light the place of your
>   coming and your going.
>
>   "Epitaph for a Poet"

"The twenty-fifth hour of the day" nicely characterizes the relationship of poetic time to ordinary time—no problem for the reader. "The wings of hope" is deceptively easy and indeed a cliché. But having lured us in with an easy entrance, he now proceeds with a display of utterly original imaginative pyrotechnics. The poet flies through a sort of rosy birth canal, which constitutes the halfway house of the bardo that is now being constructed. In that place the gray stars have not yet wakened, the only light is from the poet's own sun, and in it he can hear the bells of the underworld whose ringing seems like the sound of the poet's own poetry, being read aloud by a tearful eulogist quoting an unwritten speech by him—a speech whose subject is the beat of the mitral valve as it sends the last rush of blood throughout the dying body. But that valve is also an eyelid, the eyelid of the world's horizon, whose blinking lights up the place of dying and being born.

Now surely this is quite over the top. It's a royally mixed metaphor that the *New Yorker* would instantly condemn. But as the reader follows the poet through the maze, trusting—as he or she must—the clue or thread of its logic, the mental and emotional twists and turns of it engender precisely that mixture of ghastly terror, vertiginous freedom, solemn awe, and weird joy that a true grasp of death can produce.

Much contemporary poetry is ruthlessly tasteful and restrained, all being done by delicate little shades of meaning and ethical reflections (or is just brutally direct). By comparison, Marinaj is the master of outrageous hyperbole, of spectacular verbal pyrotechnics. His vocabulary, ranging across centuries of dictions and a gamut of scientific disciplines, his tones ranging within the same stanza from grand tragedy to hilarious irreverent wit, his shameless philosophical speculations, his subjects embarrassingly intimate and unembarrassedly sublime, break into the poetry workshop world like Cossack cavalry into a garden party. He takes the liberties offered by the more adventurous forms of current literature—Latin magic realism, Eastern European surrealism, and science fiction—and raises the ante. But it is not a mere succession of associations, as in "language poetry." There is a thread, a logic, but it is hyperbolic in its shape.

Hyperbole: hyper-bolein. Throwing-beyond. A Marinaj poem is like a rocket, ballistic at its apogee and maneuverable in all directions once it is in free fall. Expect this from Marinaj. The reader must give away his or her bashfulness. And then sometimes the poetry will suddenly become shockingly and movingly simple, the simplicity and vision of the world earned by the wild ride of the takeoff.

Perhaps Marinaj's life prepared him for his peculiarly adventuresome practice of writing. Or was it the other way round? Marinaj grew up in a remote mountain town in northern Albania, a world of farmers and shepherds not much different from that of Homer—indeed, the oral epic tradition still survived, and Gjekë's own farmer father was an oral poet.[2] Even in the oppressive era of Enver Hoxha and his successors Gjekë's literary talents were recognized, but the real break happened when, in an act of supreme youthful courage, he published a poem, "Horses," in the national literary journal. Everyone in Albania—except at first the government censors—recognized it as a satire on the oppressive regime. Someone tipped off the censors. Marinaj escaped on foot over the mountains into Yugoslavia pursued by government

---

2. Marinaj and I collected and translated a body of oral poems from recordings of the *guslers*, or poem singers of Malësia. It was published under the title *Sung across the Shoulder: Heroic Poems of Illyria* (Richardson, TX: Mundus Artium Press, 2011).

goons with dogs and guns. But the damage had been done, and when the regime was overthrown a few years later, the crowds of protestors in the squares were chanting his lines. Marinaj was and is also a hero for Kosovo and several other Balkan countries in their struggle for independence.

The geste of his life, then, was to cross the boundary of his world and thus to help transform his world itself. This is the epic work of hero and poet—to reveal the world we live in as a game by playing the game for life-and-death stakes and speaking of that which one must, as Ludwig Wittgenstein put it, remain silent. But it is only one who knows the true value of the game itself who can constructively add to it. He is not a merely revolutionary poet. There is nothing cheaply oedipal about his journey. Marinaj is as pious as Aeneas, even when he recognizes that his poetic vocation must set him apart from the dear family who gave him the life and soul of a poet, as in his crucial poem "A Book Gift from My Parents." Many of his finest poems are precisely about home, about his parents, his village and his neighbors, and they are full of that Homeric yearning for Nostos, for the smells and kindness of home. Of his neighbors in his home village of Brrut he writes:

> When I was a child
> I flew to their arms like a snowbird;
> always I found welcoming birdsong
> in the endless white fields of their hearts,

and the sweet smell of fritters
in the fresh air of the morning. . . .

. . . As one of the dead
often when I die
I find myself, arms crossed, inhumed behind their
    eyelids;

And my neighbors open their eyes
and I rise again.

> "My Neighbors in Brrut"

Marinaj has been an exile, a refugee. He is one of many Albanians who have lost and yearned for a home to which they cannot return, even when the political and practical barriers are down, for the true exile is not in space but time. Some of his poems deal movingly with this condition. But they also contain a larger implication, that the poet speaks for all humans, who are always crossing the border of the present from the realm of their past home into the strangerhood of the future. The poem itself is the tent that the wanderer puts up against the rain, or like the newspaper or the map of the immigrant in this wonderful little poem:

The Secret of the Immigrants

Their lives are tucked seriously under their arms
like yesterday's yellowed newspaper.

Bravely they fly with the wind like fog.

> They scribble maps forever
> till comets become their human antennas;
>
> become the ticktock of world philanthropy.

The other side of exile is the wide world that it opens. Marinaj is a great traveler, and his poems and his presence have shown to many nations their own faces truly seen. He has been honored in over a dozen countries as a great poet and ambassador of peace; this collection is the first in English, but he has been translated into many languages, including Romanian, Serbian, German, Italian, Russian, Vietnamese, Azerbaijani, Uzbek, Korean, French, Lao, Bengali, and Spanish. His poems on Mount Fuji, the Blue Nile, Vietnam, the romantic cities of the Balkans, Mexico, and the United States turn them into dwelling places and homes. Most compelling of all his celebrations of the planet is his mini epic of India, which I will revisit at the end of this introduction.

Marinaj is known for his delightful love poetry, with its combination of tender feeling, self-mockery, and insight into that peculiar emotion. In a poem recalling his younger days as a heartthrob of northern Albania he falls into a passion of jealousy at the liberties the sea is taking with his beloved as she swims:

> Because one day I saw you with the sea.
>
> His powerful muscles
> sucked you into his chest.

He kissed your eyes
as if they were the first eyes
he'd ever seen.
For a few seconds, even,
you forgot to breathe.
and I too forgot
to fill my chest with air, as you did.

You floated off into his bluish chest
like a white angel.

Yes, yes, I watched you with the sea
while he stretched out his water fingers
(just to make me mad),
softly touched your hair and face;
like a sly snake he reached around
and under your swimsuit—

And you knew very well, didn't you,
that those were the things I should have been
 doing with you.
Yes, yes! What you did with the sea
you should have done only with me.

    "Because One Day I Saw You with the Sea"

Here he is frankly laughing at himself, and we laugh with him at ourselves too. But together with these poems that both celebrate and make fun of Grabuta, the Albanian love goddess, Marinaj's oeuvre also contains one of the most powerful extended records of the love of a husband for his wife in the history of poetry. Dusita is an expert ICU nurse, and during the COVID-19 pandemic they had to contemplate the possibility of infection:

Another One on COVID-19

If COVID-19 strokes you, I demand
that I may share its prickly spikes with you,
not just through your angelic healing hand,
but your diviner soul and body too.

As you breathe life into the almost dead,
love is your best and surest PPE;
if life were but for one, not to be shared,
then life here was not made for you and me.

We'll use each other's lungs for ventilators,
compassion's breath will circulate between;
the gods will smile on us, their emulators,
at one of heaven's two gates we'll enter in:

either up there among the rainy skies,
or down here in this world of tears and sighs.

Some of Marinaj's most important poems deal with death, or rather with the traditional idea of the underworld and the ritual bardo that humans require to navigate it. The poems included in the "Acheron" section are the ones that most directly address the theme. Marinaj comes from a Catholic background (which is alluded to in his poems on Skanderbeg, one of the heroes of Christian resistance against Ottoman oppression and enslavement), but his theology is entirely his own. He is, I would suggest, a spiritual naturalist; that is, he does not require a supernatural realm of ghosts and disembodied spirits, but finds in nature—its extraordinary evolutionary history, and its emergent human dream—miracles and divinities enough. The dead are with us not as abstractions but as stubborn features of the concrete world. Marinaj is deeply attracted to the polytheism of India, as evidenced in his mini epic, and the existence of saints like Mother Teresa is for him ample evidence for divine purpose in the planet's exploratory journey. Though Marinaj reverences Plato, it is as a worthy opponent rather than a prop or master.

Human evil itself is to him proof of the existence of hell. The underworld he suggests in "On the Ferryboat of Acheron" is already here, in our political and personal crimes:

> Into this fetid dungeon
> —Of course—
> Blow the suffocating ashes of hell's dead,
> Declaring the latest fashion
> Of the madness of the ancients.
>
> There the instinctive hammer of the obscurantist
> Hammers to an edge the grudge
> Against the human trafficking
> In the migration of the dead.

> Demons project the future
> Of the civilization above the ground:
>
> A book must be found
> Older than the Bible
> That maps the geography of a new civilization
> As a great oven covered by a gray silken canopy
>   of ash.
>
> There hell is,
> Forever part of the existing geography,
> Maintaining the ghetto walls
> That channel the flowing river
> Of the spirits of the dead.

Marinaj's vision of the city of the underworld derives from Virgil's and Dante's. In "My Conversation with Death," he anticipates his own death journey and offers his soul as fuel to light the streets of the necropolis.

> One day you'll take me by the hand,
> Simply, without asking.
> Two black globes heavily will drop
> To replace my eyes.
> Two night-sharp telescopes you will hang
> Upon my cold neck.
> Two lives further you will push my body
> Away from myself.
>
> You will call all these
> A personal experience.
> You will convince me that I left

Just to create a theory . . .
You will label my complaints
As expressions of a subjective point of view.

As for my soul—
In the cressets of the ancient city
You will burn it up
Where it will flare like neon.

People will promenade
Through the labyrinths of all the old motivations
Turning my emotions
Into trottoirs where footfalls make no sound.
I will pay for my sins—
For all those unwritten poems
And for the girls that in the name of morality
Left their love for me to die.

For Marinaj, death is related to morality as a sort of retroactive ennobling—death casts backward in time a grandeur of meaning that we can sense, in our highest moments, and that in turn can help us make our dying into a poem.

Marinaj's poetry refuses to run crying to authority or faith in supernatural power to justify right action and condemn human crime. The poet's task here is not to weaponize the evil of others for moral or political or ethnic or sectarian advantage, but to see and name and make us see it as it is. He puts irony to its best use, revealing without comment the self-justifications of the oppressor. In the section titled "Admonitions," he takes up the traditional role of poet in calling out and rightly naming the cruelty and ugliness of power, whether embodied in persons or in political machines, tribes, and governments. But in his voice there is no political correctness, no partisan mendacity—as if he is able to take off (or rather never put on) the spectacles of media labeling and see events fresh and without prejudgment.

To understand Marinaj's sense of both personal and political morality, it is essential to grasp his vision of the work of the poet. He does not, as many poets do, regard poetry as the servant of morality, but as the source of it. He regards true poets as prophets, upstream from the philosophical and theological codifiers of ethics, and even further upstream from political ideology and factional and personal self-interest. His elegy for Neruda is explicit:

> As an open champagne bottle boils
> the waves spit white foam from their mouths
> and mermaids dance about the lyrics of the poet
>
> an old waltz borrowed from the Corybantes
> to the music Mozart composed in secret
> as an anthem for the true artists of Paradise,
> this time for Ricardo Eliécer Neftali Reyes
> > Basoalto,
> whom even the Atlantic has accepted as deeper
> > than itself.
>
> > "With Neruda on the Atlantic Shore"

Not that the poet is detached from reality. Rather, the poet speaks from what T. S. Eliot called a unified sensibility, a view that takes in all the levels of voluntary being: the animal, the sensory, the emotional, the rational, and the spiritual, and embodies them in the natural symbology of the world. Morality is for him a crude diagram of that deeply empathic understanding. Marinaj does not demonize evil people, but mourns that they have demonized themselves, and understands them from the inside suffering their own hell. In "The Kronoses of the Twentieth Century," he experiences the anguish of the genocide workers who find they can never bury all the accumulated dead:

> Millions we sent through Hades' gates;
> we had become their Cerberus:
> they come back tens that went in eights,
> like phoenixes from Erebus.
>
> Do such reactions do much good,
> dear chemists, physicists, and fiends?
> replace with poison children's blood:
> why keep them living by such means?
>
> Why let them reach the age of hell?
> They're gunpowder, they'll never cease,
> just like their parents—might as well
> dispatch them now to live in peace. . . .

One of the signs of Marinaj's unified sensibility is his embrace of scientific concepts and vocabulary.

Not for him the usual poetic disdain for science that ranges from amused curiosity to outright blame for all the ills of our "materialistic" age. Marinaj has had a scientific education as well as a humanistic one and is at home in the ways we humans have penetrated and been penetrated by the mysteries of nature. Like Johann Wolfgang von Goethe and Samuel Taylor Coleridge, his curiosity sets itself no limits.

The long poem that concludes this volume exemplifies the comprehensiveness of his vision. *The Lost Layers of Vyasa's Skin*—I italicize its title because it is a book in itself—is a remarkable achievement, five epic quests rolled into one: a wildly metaphorical account of a poetic pilgrimage through India, an ethical search for a cure for our deeply troubled world in the footsteps of the Albanian saint we know as Mother Teresa, a phantasmagorical journey under the ocean that goes to the root of our current ecological crisis, a poetic reconciliation of Western and Eastern moral theologies, and a description of his own spiritual initiation as a poet.

It is a unique work, certainly in the epic tradition but using epic freedoms and affordances to explore ideas and experiences that are beyond the bounds of what had been sayable. Perhaps the closest analogues might be Dante's *Divine Comedy*, Arthur Rimbaud's *Le Bateau Ivre*, and Coleridge's *Rime of the Ancient Mariner*.

As his translator I am honored to introduce Marinaj to the Anglophone world. The reader, I believe, will find in his work flavors and perspectives that are radically new, but that are strangely reminiscent—perhaps of some of those earliest synesthetic experiences we had as children, before ordinary language dissected them into abstract categories; experiences as delightful as they are sometimes disturbing.

Self-Portrait

Marlowe graced me with Faustus; now I perceive
more exactly the value of spirit, the cost of
    knowledge;
more clearly I see now the curved line of the
    equator
and the human-animal graft of the centaur.

The vision of the culture of suffering,
the deconstruction of the atom's secret nucleus,
to know the chemistry of the explosive, and the
    results of the explosion—

these still remain my offensive strategy,
my defense system against the gas's detonator.

*

Exhausted by keeping watch on paper alone
I have built myself out beyond the bounds of my
    body,
beyond the holy water squeezed out of Philip Sidney
that made him murmur, "Thy need is greater than
    mine."

With irises written less densely yet than their whites
my eyes drive the world into logic's antipodes,
around the dangerous balance of love and pain.

I rise and fall with the planet Kiçelev,[3]
careful not to desecrate the moon footprints of the
 astronaut.

*

My atmosphere is a thin layer of life and death,
its hemisphere's core remains one of sweat and
 blood,
its biosphere guides my neurons to connect,
helping the lithosphere guard my face from shame.

I have nothing to confess to the dark laws of chaos,
I abhor the effects of any prelude to invasion,
the destruction of even one person for the good of
 another.

Forgive me, Milton, but it were better
to serve in heaven than rule in hell.
Teach Me How to Whisper

---

3. Reverse of Veleçik, a mountain in northern Albania.

Home

My Neighbors in Brrut[1]

When I was a child
I flew to their arms like a snowbird;
always I found welcoming birdsong
in the endless white fields of their hearts,

and the sweet smell of fritters
in the fresh air of the morning.

As a young man
I flew like one of Shiroka's[2] swallows
into a landscape
where doves protect you from predators,
where mannequins undo one button,
(a proposal that I resist),
despite the pains of every feeling—love, logic, reason.

But still
in the wicker hut of my ribcage,
folded in the yellowing pages of old books
I find and find again my neighbors' transparent love.

As a man,
it seems I have almost forgotten the way back to
    Brrut.

---

    1. Birthplace of Marinaj in Malësia e Madhe.
    2. Filip Shiroka: important Albanian renaissance poet. The reference is to a poem of his about migrating swallows.

I don't cry,
because there are "thoughts too deep for tears,"
but I always knock on their open doors,
though the blackberry thorns bloody my hands.

As one of the dead
often when I die
I find myself, arms crossed, inhumed behind their
    eyelids;

And my neighbors open their eyes
and I rise again.

My Home in Brrut

From the house where I was born in Brrut now pour
childhood memories that sprinkle over my face:
milked from poetic teats that only I know how to
    draw.
Half sorrowful, half brilliant with ancient grace,

Still those days like oracle birds flush forth from me
out of the turbulent years of my first growing,
calling me with an imperious urgency
to be among humans always a human being.

From the roof of that house my earliest dreams took
    flight:
now it remains, tired witness of my first campaign,
the castle where defending poetry I fight
the long war of life; falling, getting up again.

The Lullaby Singers

For the farmers

They step into the golden fields and turn at once
into men of iron. The midday heat

Gurgles in their souls. They rub their hands
that rasp like the ploughshare

Down the furrow. The earth shakes and murmurs
under their feet, as they become the singers

Of lullabies. It would be no wonder
if one day we might hear the very cobs themselves

Sprout from their human veins.
The soil's warmth causes their blood

To bubble, which is why they have no fear
of the open spaces, the gray soil, or the turbid water

The color of weak coffee. The rippling muscles of
    the earth
don't raise calluses on hand or face.

As the sun shrinks their shadows
into shorter men, they take part in a new waltz,

the threshers of the earth.
they slice the heat into slips of paper

and shake into them the dust of their faces
for a smoke. The sweat, like a comic barmaid,

puts out their cigarettes. Before they join
in the birdsong, they turn their fingers into rakes

to give the earth a final comb.
The tiredness melts unaware through their fingers

and dribbles away with ease like the snow in August
branding their names on the earth's soft cheeks.

And then the sun gently shakes his head above them
as it stoops down under the heavy breathing of the
    night.

The First Kisses of Nature

Don't fear the flowers, come now in a rush,
have made the pure dawn blush:

their soft lip-prints, scattered here and there
upon the meadow's sprouting body everywhere
are not like winter's frosty prints:
they're nature's first and freest kisses.

To set a rose upon this bosom's innocence,
such godlike loveliness as this is,
would be to snip the light in strips to blot and dry
the redness of the stars up in the sky.

On My Mother's Birthday

I just saw my mother in a dream

like a withered rose
in the hands of a saint
with sixty-two fallen petals
that have rotted into the earth.
Her head hangs in the sky of a new life
filled with black clouds
that hesitate to turn to rain.
As clean and tranquil as a lady
she wept for the first time
through my eyes;
and moistened the feather pillow
of fine down plucked from the white chickens—
slaughtered and scalded bald
and meant only for the pleasure of the guests.

How can I sleep
when the silence in the room has all steamed off?
In one ear
I hear the sound of forks and spoons
on the more fortunate ladies' tables,
but in the other
I seem to hear the grate of fork and shovel,
my mother working in the fields.
Oh, I know men shouldn't cry
(that's what my mother used to tell me)

but the hardship of her life still wounds me to the
 soul:
she is far too young to die
and far too tired to live.

Anthem for My Parents

My ascension in the world
is just a wisp of steam
to warm their callused fingers:
twenty pilled and knotted walking sticks
joined to make for me
a heavenly baby walker made of love.

I could be considered a crinkle
of balled-up writing paper,
the space between two stanzas of a song,
the smell fresh ink leaves when you scratch it off.

But who I am, to tell the truth,
can always be found planted deep
in the soil under the fingernails
of their hard work.

May 1, 2006

Ode to My Parents

How many heavy loads have they borne,
backs bowed like the arches of bended bows,
and still their eyelids open and close
like an old book jacket, worn and torn,
on a diary of legends that nobody knows.

This century's melting like snowflakes in their
    palms,
as if with a guilty conscience shrinking before their
    gaze;
they found little beauty in it, with all its charms,
but for those seven children like seven clear bright
    days.

They've tried to wave the century good luck in their
    disappearance,
as if they'd rubbed out all the bitterness of its ways
with their golden eraser made of silence and
    endurance.

A Book Gift from My Parents

> *(My father, angry at me for neglecting the harvest because I was reading, took the book away and told me he would only give it back after five years.)*

Unwrapped, the classic Greek anthology
still bore upon its covers marks or brands
of mud and nervous fingerprints that he,
my father, left on from his work-stained hands.

And here, like two smudged hemispheres, there dwelt
two teardrops that concealed what went unsaid:
my mother thus unraveled what she felt,
a silence broken like spider thread.

A five-years' sentence, with his old whetstone
locked in his tool chest, the book speechless lay,
because at the wrong time I read alone
as the rain danced upon the drying hay.

Maybe the value lost by my inaction,
saved might have bought a pan of hot cornbread
to fill seven children's tums to satisfaction
when dreams and hunger vied there to be fed.

The Sphinx-like pages of the book were gnawing
the time I should have spent on fields of bread,

—bread of his dust and sweat, his sowing,
    mowing—
deaf to the waltz of rain where hay lay spread.

I'd bought the book without his due permission,
that book I riffle now through all their days,
as if I threshed there all their pains and passion,
two miracles, alike, that still amaze.

While with fine nerves their life was weaved and fed,
of breath my love of reading was, its strife;
they saw the pages as the rounds of bread:
I saw the pages as the rounds of life.

They're the front and back covers of my life.

Albania

The Highlanders of Malësia e Madhe

Invading storm clouds,
like the beards of old butchers
steeped in blood,
think they can drop in at the *sofra*[1]
to drink a fathom of light
from the sun of the highlanders' eyes.

They smell like a butchery,
so Malësors[2] hold their chins an ell above the clouds.

---

1. *Sofra*: traditional Albanian village dining table.
2. Malësor: a citizen of Malësia e Madhe, the mountainous north of Albania.

The Return of Skënderbeu[1]

The undone
stitch
in that black mantle
that Vojsava had knitted

was clue enough
not just to find
the way back home,

but also to embroider
a black eagle
on his breast

before transplanting it
forever

onto both sides
of the red flag of Albania.

---

1. Skënderbeu (or Skanderbeg): nickname of Gjergj Kastrioti, the legendary hero who, sent as a child hostage to serve as a Janissary, remembered his home nation and returned to fight for it as a rebel against the Ottoman Empire. Vojsava was his mother.

Skënderbeu's Advantage

Gjergj Kastrioti was more than a single neuron
In the brain of the century of wonders.
He didn't read the scale of the map's borders,
He never pronounced a lifeless moment dead.

His thoughts were half his, half his parents',
Well-meditated in the neurons' collectivity.
He trained to direct his impulses.
He won
With an army of unknowing individuals
Consistent with the old philosophy
Of the staves that, separated, broke.

Since the Time They Killed Omer

A legendary Albanian hero

The week stopped at seven days since the time they killed Omer.
The anguished sighs of noblemen lopped off the heads of mountains
and turned the soil into fog and rocks into clouds.
Even now Aikuna[1] calls out to her son to rise from the grave:
Arise, arise, oh my son!
Without you life is . . . not life . . .

A willow stands alone on the mountain of Jutbine.
Halil[2] planted it at the head of Omer's grave to be a mother to him.
Muji[3] thundered—aching with pain, he thundered.
(And the heavens preserved his peal of thunder
to herald the imminence of rain, and hail . . .)
The son was soaked by the mother's tears.
    Curses! . . .
A message from his heart then did he graft
into the care-laden willow fronds
that hung above his brother's head.

    1. Aikuna was Omer's mother.
    2. Albanian folk hero.
    3. Albanian folk hero.

(See the willows, how they weep!)
And as a man of flame, in lightning he was
 immortalized.

The Fortune-Teller[1]

My homeland was turned upside-down
like an unwashed coffee cup:
the grounds, according to the fortune-teller
thousands of empty dead-end streets.
It always goes this way
when you have more faith in the fortune-teller than yourself.

---

1. Composed in 1997, the date of the chaotic political turmoil that nearly resulted in a civil war in Albania.

Why Do You Look at Me Like That?

Friends, pals,
why do you look at me like that?
I know.
My past is one long adventure.
But I had nothing to lose
going to America.

Going to America
I could lose everything.

Bubbles in the Adriatic

> *In memory of the Albanian emigrant ship* Katëri i Radës, *wrecked in the Strait of Otranto at the southern end of the Adriatic Sea with the loss of eighty-three lives, March 28, 1997.*

South in both senses.
Specific gravity:
salt and Albanians,
water and death.

Black mourning and imaginary paradises,
bouquets with no grave to lay them on,
the lowered eyes and voice of the twilight.

Testaments drowned in the slapping waves
forbade any kiss on the forehead.
Tears shattered the laws of space.

The Siberian emblem
on the handcuffs of Dostoevsky[1]
is the only map of the graves of the drowned.

The master compulsions of illusion,

---

1. Fyodor Dostoevsky was shackled and sent to Siberia for his views.

demons with reptile bodies,
myths that freeze evenings into statues—
realities that blow tears
into unending bubbles upon the Adriatic.

Lament

> *My grandmother mourns the loss of the Albanian emigrants*

You left your things so you could travel lighter.
You left your kids so they could stay sincere.
You left the poverty to not die as a pauper.

You chose the frowning sky's life after death.
You fought the crazy seas beyond all fear.
You lost yourselves where you would find yourselves.

You left your souls collateral for your debts.
You left your houses silent, dead, and drear.
You bit your bitter tongue until it bled.

You scratched fate in the face to save the others.
I know this half-dead mourner gives no cheer.
But what this cry means for Albania!

The Secret of the Immigrants

Their lives are tucked seriously under their arms
like yesterday's yellowed newspaper.

Bravely they fly with the wind like fog.

They scribble maps forever
till comets become their human antennas;

become the ticktock of world philanthropy.

Yesterday

I milked
the white breasts
of the Mountains
of Rejection.

So I
can invite a friend or two

for at least
a cup of milk and snow.

Hoping to Find Refuge in America[1]

For we who still think patient means hopeful,
morning is a balm
for eyes bruised with black footprints of night.

We breathe with the ease of saplings in a breeze
and fill our rotted lungs with hope.
We build our airy rooftops
upon the heart's high peaks
and cover them at once
with wretched shreds of secrecy.

We declared ourselves dead refugees.

All the cares of the world are etched
on the dark globes of our eyes;
our hearts are powerless
to signal the message of their decease.

Our frozen visions
drip down like icicles on either side of life and death.

We are a quilt of dreams
embroidered with the tragedies of the days,
and wait in angst and hope

---

1. In 1991 Marinaj was in a refugee camp in Serbia, awaiting a permit to enter the United States.

for humankind to surface from the depths
in all its splendor.

Unlike America,
time loses its integrity here
on the brink of the grave.

Without Immunity

I found Albania like a white angel
walking slowly one span above the ground
among the shades of the dead with bouquets in their hands.

I hugged them to me, with a pale wounded face
like an orange with bite marks in it.

I saw its fingers stained with dried blood,
still painful where the nails had been pulled out
to serve as tiles upon the icy pyramid.[1]

I shrank and became the oil of Albania's lamp
and merged into the wick with its gray head of snuff.

I felt my burning leave images of ash.
But though the light I gave looked dim and smoky
all eyes froze to glass about me, that it be not put out.

If I had spiritual immunity in Albania,
shameless, I'd keep to myself the salt of my tears.

Tirana, June 2006

---

1. Popular name of the former Enver Hoxha Museum, nicknamed "the pyramid."

To Shkoder[1]

No, don't close yet the windows of this evening,
let my emotions thunder in your sky;
like migrant birds who fly in grief, they sing,
"Shkoder, Shkoder"—but it's in vain they cry.

Don't light the candles of the dark tonight,
Or bring to dine Rozafa's[2] patient pain;
my yearning's fire enough to set alight
and dress with the bright sun your urbane moon.

Spread out your theater's wings—as once they flew—
and you the bird between them, high and free;
Migjeni,[3] who bit more than he could chew,
shall dry your tears with my soft poetry.

---

1. Shkoder: city in northern Albania, former capital.
2. Rozafa: Albanian tragic heroine. According to a legend, three brothers wanted to build a castle, but the walls kept collapsing. An old man told the brothers that if they wanted the castle to stand, they had to bury alive in the walls whichever of their wives brought them food the next day, but they couldn't tell them beforehand. The two older brothers broke this promise and told their wives what would happen. The youngest one kept the secret, and his wife, Rozafa, brought the food. After learning the story, Rozafa accepted immurement, but only if part of her body, including her right breast, remained free enough to feed her infant son.
3. Migjeni: Millosh Gjergj Nikolla, Albanian poet who died tragically at twenty-six years old. Shkoder's Migjeni Theater was famous for its fine wings and curtains.

Wounded stars fill nostalgia's midnight sky;
when it is night here, there it is the day.
You wring your feelings out, and I am dry;
your grandeur soaks me, though, and heals my grief
    away.

With My Head in the Lap of Kosovo

To those who died there

Humanity has antennae of compassion
and we are surely more than self-reflection
as we follow the new rhythms that arise at midnight.

Ask me as your son for the compassion
I feel when I lay my head in your lap
and hate no one.

Learn how your presence makes me feel more than
 a man,
one who fights always to end a war,
follow, let us share our griefs together.

As when a lethal abstraction flies over us
and we squeeze together into a neutral zone awaiting
our new strengths as a chance of healing.

How can we let mere numeric probability
defeat the promise of the word
while the map of death still haunts us?

Then, that we might exercise the antennae of
 compassion,

let our new anthem—a clear music
like stars threaded upon the nerves—

be blown by the western winds
into the wounds of war.

Let us return, and save us from ourselves
by turning into energy all our weapons
and all our energy into the guardian of human love.

The Balance

> *On the eighth anniversary of Marinaj's parting from Albania*

Eight years
swallowed like eight aspirins
we never stop
running after the human axis
all our lives defeated by life's own formula.

Riddle

Whenever I pray for Albania
I borrow the language of the Ave.

I calculate on my fingers.

I think God
speaks with Albanians only at night.

I believe fanatically

that life is like Homer's eyes
and on death I agree with Dante.

    Who am I?

Amor

As the Dew Kisses the Mountains, but Sweeter Still

Spring makes a meadow of the Sahara under my
    feet,
greened by your grace with a fragrance of your own.
My love, we are the pollen of the touch-me-not
    flower
on the sheets that saved their virginity for us alone.

Summer fires up the Arizona under my skin
and we transpire the moisture of the air round our
    faces.
Yours—the painting God kept for himself—
is the mirage I follow always, thirsty for your oasis.

Fall in its yellowy quilt of silk
covers our spirits' love in its resurrection;
a thousand torches of feeling jet from my body
to robe with the sun the echo of your predilection.

The winter whistles an old pagan melody,
and follows you lustfully twirling his beard, until
you roll in like a smiling avalanche and lift me
as the dew kisses the mountains, but sweeter still.

**We Were Adolescents and Put off Love
until Tomorrow**

The air shook with the sounds of the city.
Beyond, the forest waited to embrace us
with its green veil.
our first encounter called for quieter places.
The sky was blue; no fog was in the offing,
it was noon, but it seemed like dusk somehow.
We hadn't touched a drop, yet we felt drunk.
How could we fathom the thirst for the unknown,
Ignore the people's hard devouring stares,
how could we trust the open spaces of the fields?
The birds eavesdropping there?
The sly glances of the sunflowers?
Wasn't it a sin to make the very leaves of the forest
yearn with longing when they looked upon us?
What if the grass, where we rioted, caught fire
from our torrid passion and burned?
Hmm? We were adolescents,
which is why we put off love until tomorrow.

Where Is the Girl?

Where is the girl who once upon a time I loved:
Veleçik would shiver when her footsteps went by.
She was the one who left Kastrat[1] blear and
    sleepless;
drunk with her white face the sun staggered in the
    sky!

Where is the girl who once upon a time loved me,
who set my feelings at war in their fiery birth,
she the divine one, who with her very first kiss
burned up the thread that bound me to the earth!

Where is the girl I loved once, the girl who loved me,
who made my blood race as if fleeing a crime,
she who with her lips' transubstantiating heat
halted and stayed that first breathing moment of
    time!

---

1. Kastrat: regional settlement in Malësia e Madhe, home of one of the seven tribes of the region.

Winter

So dry-lipped winter's icy fingers still
shake slightly as his bond is loosening . . .
he hides the boy's defeat, with a farewell
that's only ashes, in the breast of spring.

He cannot hide the season's disappointments,
Platonic feelings brewed in silencing:
his fires too weak to quell the disenchantments
that barred more entry to the heart of spring.

He shrinks within his worn sheepskin, heartbroken,
in the sky's thunder he is lost and done;
but by the spring those sickened hopes are woken,
now she disrobes, a metaphor of the sun.

But winter shuns this weeping-willow love;
he turns the seconds into laboring;
in lust's realm lost and found, but raised above,
he's taken, briefly, by the milky lips of spring.

His quavering chin abhors the laws of nature;
for winter's death means flowering for spring;
the force that slaps his face, bitter truth's teacher
wails never, never, when the cold winds sing.

She Makes the Horizon Blush

Silhouette of a girl

Something about her I tremble to outline.

A hint of pigments, polyphenols
merged into waves of velvet
spins in my head an amorous brain turbine
fitted with flattering vanes of light
and turned by an urgent flow of feeling.

Her intent glance makes fresher the moist air of the forest,
sets the sky of the skyline
into a blush of whispery incandescence.

The evening can't have fallen asleep so early!
How could the sky turn its back on her
just when the meadows are sweating a musky dew
and Roman Venus and Greek Aphrodite are green with envy

at this new goddess?

The twilight breeze has liquefied into joy,
then condensed back into a lax protoplasm
to protect her. As if I didn't exist,
while the moon's at liberty to tiptoe down

and peek in at her between the branches
of a permitting tree

like an overripe blood orange waiting to be peeled.

A segment of that almost translucent range of hills
has been turned, trembling, into a vertical image
to fit the perfect curve of her silhouette,

leaving me wondering
why the laws of nature do not prohibit such natural
    wonders,
as heartbreaking as they surely are . . .

Timorous to be within range of that distant gaze

I ask myself
how can so celestial a being
be penned, a note of music, behind that equals sign
of the iron railings at waist and knee?

One World Ocean

A snakeskin looped around my neck, you're
    evermore
squeezing and throttling me, and I know why.
Your words like lightning strike at our love's core:
"It's over for us," two suns in an empty sky.

Why? Because it lets you write again
when all your springs and veins are dry
in a forbidden desert with no rain
and no fresh water from that sky.

You hunt me with your cruel love-ending threats:
hurting me, yes, is a refreshing guilt;
it's sparks on kindling, and the fiercer it gets,
the quicker your poetic journal's being built.

For God's sake stop that stabbing with your knife
between the sixth and seventh rib, that's all.
Don't use my blood for ink, now—that's my life.
Don't dress your burnt-out heart up with the flora of
    my soul.

Don't let your feelings turn to hungry lions,
set them to forage in the grasslands of my chest.
Don't classify your lady thoughts with suchlike signs
as these: "Your voice is mine"; your own good voice
    is best.

So know my love for you is stranger, wilder hurled
than are the wave fronts of the five free seas,
deeper than secrets of the underworld:
don't think this five-branched hand can never wave
    farewell,

Though this is so much more than love, more tensed
and weighty than the one world ocean ever yet could
    fit,
purer than the sweet herbs Ophelia dispensed,
one of these days your pirate ships may sink in it.

Because One Day I Saw You with the Sea

Reflections on a memory

Back then we had no wings
to carry us to love;
we were as unfledged as two young canaries
waiting for love
to be dropped into our open mouths.

"Touches are dangerous for kids"
(you told me);
"Kisses are playing with fire.
Lovemaking
before you're properly grown up—
No way!" you said.

But it seemed that I could breathe
only through your lungs:
when I slept, you were the dream
where happiness and shaking fear
swung there in equilibrium.

When I walked, you kept me in the air
above the muddy streets of Bajzë,[1]
so as not to smirch the pants
that I had ironed especially for you.

---

1. A small town in Kastrat.

Every heartbeat
pumped your name in my blood.
Away from you
I was a man without his prescription glasses—
the colors of the universe
were blurred and tired as I was,
your image dissolved
into the *materia* of the world I cried out for.

So you and I, we were one body, one soul, one love;
if we added up our ages
we'd be exactly thirty-two years old.
"Even so," you said,
"You are too young, too young,"
and again you lied to me
that you wanted to remain untouched.

I say you lied.
Because one day I saw you with the sea.

His powerful muscles
sucked you into his chest.
He kissed your eyes
as if they were the first eyes
he'd ever seen.
For a few seconds, even,
you forgot to breathe.
and I too forgot
to fill my chest with air, as you did.

You floated off into his bluish chest
like a white angel.

Yes, yes, I watched you with the sea
while he stretched out his water fingers
(just to make me mad),
softly touched your hair and face;
like a sly snake he reached around
and under your swimsuit—

And you knew very well, didn't you,
that those were the things I should have been doing
    with you.
Yes, yes! What you did with the sea
you should have done only with me.

Well, how could I have known, being so young,
that if you leave lovemaking for later
it grows cold.

In the Incubator of Grabuta[1]

Swab out that one tender spot of your tyranny
with that lump of flesh you scratched from me.

Though the germs it kills will never reanimate
we have already endured the miracle of survival;

most of all when the fever of hope
leaps two degrees just by your being there.

My true love is not this discarded vision,
this anachronism of desire,

this subjection to a dream,
Nor faith's return from the realm of obscurantism.

My mornings cannot offer the kerchief of light,
though the breeze does not disdain to embrace you.

My verse beneath your girlish skin
gives and receives such melancholic metaphors.

But do not multiply the guilt by the number of the pains
that have mounted up in these two decades;

---

1. The Malësian folk goddess of love. *Gra-buta* = "ladies-gentle" in dialect.

While you fill your lungs with their effects
I ignore the syllables you whisper in our waltz;

in vain have I held your head between my hands
like a seashore disappointed with the mermaid's
    magic.

She Brought Cancun to Its Knees[1]

Aphrodite, the one and only Aphrodite,
wrapped in the sheerest silk of the moon,
leapt out of the lap of night into Cancun.

When the white sand
hugged her footprints to its chest,
dolphins sang in a higher key,
sharks took to pulling out each other's teeth,
waves held their breath.

The moment they spied her,
the sky became a verdant countryside,
shores angled their shoulders to her shape.
the earth drizzled a thin sweat,
bouquets of flowers blossomed from her breast.

Her beauty brought Cancun to its knees,
the faces of the pale waves blushed crimson,
the horizon blazed in red-hot embers,
the sun, as if drunk, shook off its rays.

Aphrodite wrung out the blue velvet cloak of the sea
and hung it swirling out to dry before her dazzling
    eyes,
then waved Cancun an insatiable goodbye
and flew into the twilight's flaming arms.

    1. Also known under its earlier title, "Aphrodite."

Your Eyes

Oh, your eyes—

they've made my verbs talk to themselves
in the sign language of divination.
They're thinning down the soporific
of the cradle's lullaby,
they bring on the expiration of my patience.

Those eyes—their side effects
include this blush that's come to the cheeks of my
    intelligence,
this defeat to my resistance against time.

Your eyes enforce
surreal dreams
that turn into poetic sentences
under the eyelids of the human anthem.

Twenty-Four Hours of Love

Twilight had sensed our need to seek out a hiding
 place somewhere,
it melted everything down to the color of chocolate,
silently giggled, seeing the red-hot blush on our
 faces,
and chanted a secret prayer for us on its way out.

In nature, naturally, we made love by nature.

In the meadows early we sweated the first dew of the
 dawn,
with the silky tresses of night we wiped the chest of
 the day,
we ripped up the flowering fields like a bolt of
 tapestry,
and found the newest, freshest smile of the Milky
 Way.

Naturally, by nature, we made love in nature.

Damn! The people who dwell in the wind had all
 somehow got word;
Mercury left the sky and dived suddenly into the sea,
the sun put his hands on his hips and stood there to
 gawk at us,
and to the earth's old muscles revealed this mystery.

By nature, we made love in nature, naturally.

Unconcerned for the desperate comets panting up yonder,
at once, like a flowery honey-drenched dream, the bold
new evening entered, and undid the top two buttons of her black shirt,
and for us she hung on her neck the moon washed in gold.

Dusita[1]

The planets suffer no harm
in their tipsy revolutions.

From the quaint standpoint of humanity
they seem equidistant, indifferent,

majestic, like the pyramids.
But they are staggered nonetheless

by the candor of your beauty;
they cast off the weariness of age

like a silk scarf, eager to behold themselves
in the mirrors of your sunrise eyes:

the planets blaze there, as beads about your throat
aglow with your healing bloom.

Looking out from where I stand,
straddling the gap between being a man

And elected by fate to be your husband,
I find it odd that on earth

humans don't identify you with the will of Venus,
don't liken you to the lights in the sky.

1. Marinaj's wife of thirty-two years.

They send up probes and astronauts
seeking life in other atmospheres,

quite unaware that something magical occurred
when you were born,

and that all those lights are aligned
to hang as ornaments around your neck.

Purgatory: An Obsolete Ballad

For Françesca and Gjovalin[1]

She was a fresh violet
waiting to bloom at dawn.
He was her lover.

They didn't call to mind
how Francesca fell in love with Paolo.

They didn't read each other any of the tale
of Lancelot and Guinevere
and found themselves in a forbidden love.

That intimate mystery between them
had no relation to the love style of Arthurian
    romance.

And so their feelings
overbrimmed.
and they imagined that society
would draw no parallels
with the first kiss of Lancelot and Guinevere.

And why should they care who spied on them?

---

1. Lovers known to Marinaj who suffered from the injustice of society.

Something beautiful and innocent
society murdered in them
before they had a chance
to ask love for absolution.

Even Dante spread no light
upon their drama,
nor did he depict it
among the exemplars of tragic romance.

The punishment of the innocent
was out of synchrony with the true sinners.
Nobody came forth as witness
to explain the sufferings
of these two delicate souls
in the court of themselves.

They say truth should not be punished
because the rituals
should never depart from public sympathy.

People ignored the drop
of the black curtains
in the ancient theaters
that cut them off from the right
to enjoy the most ordinary laws of nature.

For them the role of reputation
and respectability

erased the divine essence that burned
like a candle in the word love.

Almost everything in life about them
reflected on them an image of the pain of love,
wrung out into deformity—
the fruit of their maimed love.

They were so human
that the true sinner would pity their "sin."

For them
it were better Dante should have held back the
    Divine Comedy
till they had added another circle to the Purgatorio.

Reading Poetry with My Sweetheart

Winter: Telluride, Colorado

A selection of poems
between two hearts
that beat with the rhythm of the lines.

The night is as white as the pages,
the moonlight tinted by the fire of the words.

As we sit together on this love seat

with blown pine needles the wind
writes love's calligraphy upon the snow.

We Are Born to Love

Let the kisses fly free
in the green meadows of youth's passion,
in the cloudless skies of love.

They're the required catalysts
to clean the air we breathe.

Kisses are wonders
where the blinking eyelids of day and night
for me and you, dear fellow lovers,
turn into the barometer that marks
the shrinking time between our pulses.

For the scales of justice itself
are always figured as with open arms.

The lips are the hands of love. Often their imprints
dance between our palpitating heartbeats.

And what of us? Where do we figure in love?
I'd say this:
it is to choose the universal singularity.

Where does love figure in us, then?
it's the reason for existence,
it's the unique satellite that transmits only sincere
    voices,

it's the space where smiles and tears intercept each
    other,
it's where kisses become the voice of the future's
outstretched wings.

A Dawn with Two Suns

Today there will be no conditions for loving,
for my eyes will be seeing the world through your
      eyes,
passion sweats the must of its wine from the
      pressing,
each of our hearts turns to joy, and it flies, it flies.

That's the sun there—and see, here's you too, both
      shining;
I touch your face as the earth drowns in the
      radiance,
for love has invented new skies for our dwelling:
this dawn with its miracle, its two suns, two suns.

This morning the fresh dewdrops are soaking our
      hair,
the moment around us turns to silk, we perspire
together a coy shakiness, half joy, half fear,
we dream, we dream, lost in this nonconsuming fire.

A warm wave blushes over our faces; within
our hearts evaporates the last resisting move.
Your chest knocks at mine—mine answers, "Come
      on in."
Oh loves, loves, let our very loves themselves make
      love.

Evening

The evening veils its eyes tonight
And breathes our bodies into it.
We are two scribbles of the light,
Of all arts the most intimate.

A Freudian Moment

Id

insisted I return your unexpected kiss.

Ego

told me, "Suit yourself," and bit its lips.

Superego

put its hand on my chest:

"Don't lose the one you're already kissing."

In a Curdled Mirror

With both hands I gripped and shook the spatial illusion
like a tree loaded with melancholy oranges
and the stars fell down around my smile and withered it.

I can brew brandy enough to debauch me,
but with you away the definition of light itself has gone dead blind.
As in a curdled mirror that breaks up our love into terrains
I see a hundred faces, and don't know which one to get drunk.

Apart, we're a mere membrane between two purposes,
two convicts self-condemned to waiting,
two flowers weeping at our uprooting
from our shared field.

But I've drunk up all the brine from the ocean of longing;
I hope you never see the terrifying bottom of that seafloor's skull
where so many soft kisses have crossed their arms and perished,
so many tender touches left their clothes on the shore,

so many sweet words died in their hunger strike for
    us.

How do I find calm, to rock it in its invisible cradle,
how do I get through the cloudy tunnel of August
    without you?

I know too well the reasons, the obligations to the
    world,
but life's so short, my dearest,
we melt over it like two chips of ice
on top of a red-hot bread oven
where bake and wither the faces of our love.

Let something be left half-done, my love,
for yearning has built its cabin of embers under my
    skin
that sweats all unawares your very image.

Another One on COVID-19

*For my wife, Dusita, ICU nurse
during the first lockdown.*

If COVID-19 strokes you, I demand
that I may share its prickly spikes with you,
not just through your angelic healing hand,
but your diviner soul and body too.

As you breathe life into the almost dead,
love is your best and surest PPE;
if life were but for one, not to be shared,
then life here was not made for you and me.

We'll use each other's lungs for ventilators,
compassion's breath will circulate between;
the gods will smile on us, their emulators,
at one of heaven's two gates we'll enter in:

either up there among the rainy skies,
or down here in this world of tears and sighs.

Classi-Five

On our first meeting

I will dig new labyrinths in the art of the impossible,
when the suns of the horizons fade into drowsiness,
I'll be the valley whose echoes stay in its chest
    inaccessible,
Odysseus's arrow, touching no ring, effortless.

I will sip all the sounds of longing, of what is past
    bearing,
when to be near you the gods pray to each other;
I'll be the god who keeps death to himself, no
    sharing,
I'll be what Dickinson named herself, meeting her
    brother.[1]

I will discover the verb tenses of lightning,
leaving there in the sky for your eyes their sigil;
I'll be the last word of humanity's lullaby,
    brightening
at the focus of Michelangelo's hammer striking the
    chisel.

I will enter and riffle your dreams if you permit me
    to,

---

1. When Emily Dickinson met her fellow poet Walt Whitman, she introduced herself as "Nobody."

when your wisdom forgets to reckon the sum of my love;
I'll be the symphony Mozart did not write for you,
your lane marker, the five-lined musical stave.

As an atom recirculates all through the forms of the ordinary,
I will enrich the magic that redefines beauty,
I will add our word, *classi-five*, into the dictionary;
explain why for Adam's rib to eat of the apple was duty.

I will resurrect the hopes of the dead from their graves,
so that souls like yours will one day people the planet;
I will make a bouquet of love's labyrinthine caves,
change Shakespeare's name on his tomb to Romeo and Juliet.

Admonitions

Horses[1]

All our lives we come and go,
only see what is before us,
what's behind we fear to know,
no names are there for us;
horses, we are called.
    Do not weep,
    Do not laugh,
    Hush and heed,
    Listen up,
    Eat what we're given,
    Go where we're told:
    And none of us has got a brain.
He who was a king's horse
higher rank would hold;
he who was a princess's
saddled was with gold;
He who was a peasant's
saddled was with straw;
he who was a maverick
always slept outdoor.

And compared to humans, horses we remain!

---

1. Published in 1990, this famous poem was chanted by the crowds that brought down the dictatorial regime of Albania in 1991.

Whispering to Hiroshima

Another anniversary of the tragedy

Once more it's nature's budding time;
and so for you, as for us too, the spiderwebs of
    death
have taken their great bite out of the sun.
For we too have lain down upon your dusty bed,
leaving behind those phosphorescent prints
whose ancestry is not of one but of all peoples.

There we wipe off
the tears on both our cheeks.

Our hand of peace is not the dragon's broken claws,
nor branches to conceal a love trap's pitfall;
they are the peeled-off ribcage of a heart.

Within the pillared halls of peace
we both pronounce our condemnation,
sobbing at the hellish ruins of the twentieth century.

Your tears reflect upon our eyes,
projecting lightning shapes
on every branch of the irredeemable.

Oh, life,
life is an overwound clock, so what it strikes is
    death.

And all those deaths bury our souls with scales
where monsters of the sea still feed
somewhere in the fiery seas of that morning.

The Ambulances of Dallas

The sirens mix their bitter voices
through the streets and freeways of Dallas
where the sun sees himself in its mirrors and smiles.
In the chessboard of streets
where the games of life are played without pieces,
patients, half-computerized,
shiver like December trees,
anxious if they will live,
anxious, if they do, whether they can pay the bills.
Money doesn't grow on trees.
Billing works smoothly with invisible fingers
while the possible grabs by the throat the impossible.
Silence multiplies the screeching
as if to undo their neurochemistry:
the patients have become fiber-optic connections
whose current scratches the ceiling of their pain
and now they speak the language of trampled grass
from downturned lips like an erased opinion.
Yet in the open chess grid of the city
ambulances, ambulances, and more ambulances
cry out like the girls of Malësia shrieking to their wedding:[1]
are they healing their patients or making them sicker?

---

1. Refers to the traditional custom for Albanian girls to shriek while being transported to their wedding.

The Somali Children[1]

How can they rotate the globe
of suffering, these tiny black hands?
In this Somali wasteland
children go to sleep
wanting to dream of eating,
and they wake
like book pages swollen with wet mold.

1. Albania has its own history of colonial oppression.

A Foggy Human Dawn

This foggy morning, thinly dressed,
sits gingerly in winter's old straw rocker;
strangely the impetus of its creaking
keeps the day in the vital lead
as the Mexican Revolution kept Zapata.

Blank hours
broidered with blood, sweat, and night
try to say something calm about the crimes
from the archways where the bells are falling.

Their prophecy bleeds inside
as they see humanity refuse to be gulped down
like a glassful of wine and tears
even as it holds the waves of dream geography.

In people's shredded daily politics
words are born and drowned, like in fairy tales.
The angels with the scales of justice in their hands
fear that the earth has fallen now too far,
that humankind is out of its mind, it's too surreal
for true equality to moisten everybody's lips.

And now the leaders play "My Egg Cracks Yours."
But that egg chokes the throat of the century.

Peace at Zero

Dreams with their stubborn broom
sweep out the dust of schools that have been ground
    and crumbled
Into their blinded hands as tender as the inner
    eyelid.

The dull thudding makes my eyebrows clench.

The world's reality, like a thread on a spindle
stretched into a taut hysteric wire,
peels off the protoplasm of my cornea
and that is the only way to you, the poor, the
    unfortunate.

Through suffering our faces have become clearer
as what we are.

This trouble at my core, dear fellow humans,
sheds no light on the dark corners of my desires.
Where can I hide the two dark half circles under my
    eyes
that when united form the cipher of my peace?

Hot Air

The new century speaks

The fools are still getting doctorates in naked
 politics.
They operate in the impotent molecules of the air.

The inside of the invisible has no organs.

Shhhhh.
People are feeling my heat.
They feel my plague in their throats like a
 whirlwind.
Listen to the clinical fluids seething in their brains
as the last vestige of equilibrium seeps away.

It sounds like a lukewarm lament.

"Crutches!"
Somebody suggests crutches
so people's feet won't get burnt.
"But we have to anaesthetize the crutches."

Nobody knows that I, the fever, am the diploma
of the smartest ones who get their doctorate in
 politics.
No one will ever know
that people are my chess pieces
in the sick game of this century's maladies:

I have masked them all into shell casings,
I have promoted them all to officers, horses, and
 soldiers,
so I can remain the icon on the flag of the lost war.

Using the strategy of love I mislead the whole
 population
one by one
like snow crystals disappointed by the sun.

So those who learn to hate me lose their faith
in the game played by the breeze of unknown
 tomorrows;
but if you want to defeat me
don't search into my roots, but examine the
 molecules of the air.

The Stranger's Eyes

How unprepared they caught me!
Threaded everywhere with scarlet filaments
they seemed to me the eyes of an informer.
Not like my mother's, whose all-accepting eyes
taught me how wisely I should bless or curse;
for anyone's unknown until he's known
and always should be judged at first as good.
As poet then, I gave them the benefit.

The Darkangel

It masks the landscapes of the myths,
erases the black glyphs in the blood,

withers the desert of forgetfulness,
swallows what makes real words understood.

It purges none of Goethe's sins away,
lifts Hamlet's dark horizon high,

It versifies itself into a darkangel
condemning elegies for those who die

Eve's bite out of the apple
is life's emblem, so we're told—

The teeth marks are our Lucifer,
the promise of a perfect world.

Recurring Daymare

I watched
New York
as two
strips of
skin were
peeled from
its forehead
down to
its feet
I awoke
my face
black my
throat raw
Since that
morning my
coffee cup
steams blood
and tears.

The Kronoses of the Twentieth Century

"Say, chemists, physicists, and fiends:
what kind of formula will serve
to change the blood inside the veins
of humans while they're still alive?"

"We tried to scare their daylights out,
with red-hot chains, the clanking rack:
their bones would break, they lost their meat,
but still their blood would not turn black.

"With lead we tried their heart's extremes,
to see if the reaction worked,
their hearts rebirthed themselves in dreams:
the litmus tests lost their effect.

"We tried to roll them up in night;
why bother burying them at all?
but still they never saw the light:
gravity's apple still must fall.

"Millions we sent through Hades' gates;
we had become their Cerberus:
they come back tens that went in eights,
like phoenixes from Erebus."

"Do such reactions do much good,
dear chemists, physicists, and fiends?

replace with poison children's blood:
why keep them living by such means?

"Why let them reach the age of hell?
They're gunpowder, they'll never cease,
just like their parents—might as well
dispatch them now to live in peace.

"So wash away this Jewish blood
whose lives we eat like animals,
though we be named, now and for good,
twentieth-century cannibals."

Spit

It flies, a liquid sculpture, in an unknown arc,
compels the virtues to be relative,

Won't change its heart to any rational use,
alters no pattern of the molecules.

It is the catalyst of past atrocities,
and bans what judgement that the present offers.

Its madness tints the flames with hate,
burns up the music of the silent sources,

It pours in nature from the glands beneath the
    tongue
but turns its lenitive effect to something else.

Pointless to act as if it were a bodily fluid,
because saliva's not the same as spit.

Some of us strain, contrive to swallow it,
others just choose to spray it in your face.

If we don't understand the tragic difference,
all of our powers will vortex into violence.

Sketches in Imagination

When loss
and the charred stench of self mingle,
a man finds himself stupefied
as if marooned amongst the remnants of his dreams,
still just sketches
poorly hung in the imagination.

There, the front and back of the stage
are covered by a thin black curtain
and the least known dramas of the world
are staged by actors
while you wonder how they stole from you
the marrow of your subject, humankind!

Acheron

A Moment of Terror

The upper teeth of the sky
Are just as dangerous
As the lower teeth of the earth.

Between them

I know I will be chewed up in the end.

But I don't know what to hope for:
To be swallowed in
Or to be spat out:
Life—these dreadful jaws that own us.

On the Ferryboat of Acheron

The rivers in the kingdom of the underworld
Lower their voices for nobody,
But mumble on and on their miserable words,
Digging new arterial channels
In the naked body of the twilight.

Their messages take on life
Within the membranes of their bubbles,
Explaining for the guilty
The inscriptions in the portrait of hell:

If you are born
You are guilty.
If you can read this message
You are here.

One learns that the delta of the possibilities
Is only ever the game of a dance of pain:
That life is this:
At first an exhale, then an inhale;

Everything in between
Nothing but an opportunity
To commit sins.

But as for any natural upstanding,
And truly good deeds—on what tablet are they engraved?

According to the scriptures they are melted
Beneath the braziers of insanity,
And poured into the foaming wake
That the little ferryboat of Acheron leaves behind—

Molten in those same crucibles
As the silver obols
Extracted from the jaws of the ancient spirits
Before they are hurled into the gates of Hades.

Into this fetid dungeon
—Of course—
Blow the suffocating ashes of hell's dead,
Declaring the latest fashion
Of the madness of the ancients.

There the instinctive hammer of the obscurantist
Hammers to an edge the grudge
Against the human trafficking
In the migration of the dead.

Demons project the future
Of the civilization above the ground:

A book must be found
Older than the Bible
That maps the geography of a new civilization
As a great oven covered by a gray silken canopy of
    ash.

There hell is,
Forever part of the existing geography,
Maintaining the ghetto walls
That channel the flowing river
Of the spirits of the dead.

What was Virgil thinking
When he named hell the city of God?

"The inscriptions on these minatory gates
Portray it
As a place to confess your wrongs
And your unending contrition.

"In this place,
In this life,
Hell is the grotesque opposite of the grotesqueness
    of Paradise,
A place whence there is no escape."

My Conversation with Death

One day you'll take me by the hand,
Simply, without asking.
Two black globes heavily will drop
To replace my eyes.
Two night-sharp telescopes you will hang
Upon my cold neck.
Two lives further you will push my body
Away from myself.

You will call all these
A personal experience.
You will convince me that I left
Just to create a theory . . .
You will label my complaints
As expressions of a subjective point of view.

As for my soul—
In the cressets of the ancient city
You will burn it up
Where it will flare like neon.

People will promenade
Through the labyrinths of all the old motivations
Turning my emotions
Into trottoirs where footfalls make no sound.
I will pay for my sins—
For all those unwritten poems

And for the girls that in the name of morality
Left their love for me to die.

In the end
I will accept the furious moralist tone
Of reality,
The needles by which you shall engrave
The figure of the most important life events.
Aware
Or unaware
I will in terror honor
Your two-faced personality
And the perfection of the divine laws.

The Death of Jiva Novakovići[1]

The eyes of Jiva Novakovići,
Even those eyes of all eyes,
Like a candle burnt to ash, died out.
Their light faded more softly than the evening;
Around him hummed the dry scent of the grave.
All his good deeds, like noisy honeybees,
Swarmed in his coffin of walnut wood.
Like some amazing lacrimal agent
They brought on a contagion of weeping.
Yeah, good old Jiva is gone,
Having never understood why life is briefer
Than the body of the one who lives it.

1. Not a famous person but an everyman who lived in Socol, Romania.

The Poet's Mother Gives up the Spirit

For Luigj Çekaj[1]

The life of the poet's mother
Closed with less of a swish than an umbrella.

Her heart
For the first time
Murmured only for itself
As if it cited
A new alphabet
For prophecies of the future
Written somewhere between
The botany and the anatomy of a leaf.

As an advocate
Who has been bitten in defense of her son,
The veined blood in her hands had lost its finesse;
It was not to write any new law in this world
And froze like a poetic delta over her death.

Guiltless as Paradise itself,
Now on her face is created
A waterwheel of pain and a final smile
And once and for all she let drop on her chest

---

1. Important Albanian poet, whose mother died while he was in exile.

Like two loose Bible pages
Her honorable hands, one upon the other.

Epitaph for a Poet

You departed like a naively beautiful dream
Leaving us to fight a long war with the desire
To never wake again without you.
But you can't die, because you are a poet of the people.

For poets don't start until the twenty-fifth hour of the day
When they set out upon the wings of hope
To thread the rosy tunnel of the afterlife—
That halfway world where only poets venture:

A world waiting for the gray stars to awaken,
For it's a place that's lit up only by the poets' sun,
Where is heard only the chanting bells of the cities of the underworld
Clanging moist with tears as if reading your poems back to you,

As if they were finishing the farewell speech you never wrote,
Witnessing the way the last beat of your mitral valve
Turned to an eye whose lids are the horizons of the world
That open and close to light the place of your coming and your going.

Now is your spirit split into two halves
Like two braziers burning at the gates of life and death,
And tears crystallize into lamp chimneys to shield them from the wind
So your metaphors can be read from both sides at once.

We all find something suitable to the occasion
And as the priest's voice chatters with the chill of grief
We recite your words. And the voices of welcoming poets
Read from their side something fitting from their Babel.

Heroines

Antigone

Into the earth's last week she buried her fingers,
as into Sophocles's seven surviving manuscripts;
scrawled on the dead a word on the value of soil
and wiped out the borders set on the world map of
 love.

In return for the ripped-out smile of her brother,
 Antigone
filled up her cheeks to bursting with death and its
 dust,
and with no care for the shadings of that last breath,
blew her life out into the face of King Creon,

and spattered an image there over his godlike visage
that bore, scratched in the grave dust, that bitter
 inscription:
Who needs life when life itself is lifeless?

The Em Dash of Emily Dickinson

Nature before us yawns, an infant in the arms of
 God—
And look, a white sheet unfolds for us in the
 mountains—
We, who break the mirror between heaven and
 earth.

The hours age as they turn their thoughts to snow—
The snow ages as its flakes float thoughtful through
 the air—
I, unaware, seek out the frozen pole of your north.

Unhappy Brides

The white sheets of their dreams
tremble when they tear at the crease,
turn into bandages over the perfection of their
   vision.

Maybe they cover up the crashing waves of an
   ocean:
their girlishness lives under the veil, it lives;
in there the last flame of their voices blazes still.

However they push or pull the world of myth,
they feel as if they're burning their numbed feelings
or freezing them to insensibility.

The veil, as in a silent war zone street
moves in the air like a crippled word,
and they thin the blood of the millennium with
   every step.

The very life of those girls withers away;
within their chests' labyrinths
their volcanoes have turned explosion into a
   language.

Their hearts are like antennas over lightless roofs.
Today has died in yesterday's fog
a culture robbed of the chance to put on something
   new.

Life under the veil is a man-made eclipse,
a coffin lid over faces that still breathe,
a lost war centered between life and death.

Rozafa's Confession

Believing
a woman has less value than a man
they walled me up alive.

Thinking
it would be fed by my blood
the castle found the strength to stand.

Fearing
it might be called to witness
the River Drin[1] flowed on regardless.

Symbolizing
human self-sacrifice
they turned me into a myth.

Pretending
all these were true
I walled up murder with myself.

---

1. The Drin is a river in southern and southeastern Europe with two distributaries, one discharging into the Adriatic Sea and the other one into the Bojana River. Its catchment area extends across Albania, Kosovo, Serbia, Greece, Montenegro, and North Macedonia.

The Desperation of Desdemona

"The needle of our love
can't stay in place for long.

"Your judgement is the catalyst
that turns the reaction from its flow.

"My philosophy's credo
is that you cannot move:

"A closed circuit:
could Copernicus recant?

"Two pulls that stretch our lives' shared string:
if it's not broken yet, it's twanging tight."

Looking into Your Kind Eyes

For Elena Bujević[1]

Serenity's poetic powers
Surrender
To the fourth dimension of the twilight.

Your kind eyes sprout invisible
Blue irises
Out of the pollen of every flower.

As the waters of the baths of Vranjska[2]
Ripple,
They clear and cool, take on a new shade of love.

The breezy evening has engendered this
Translucent window
Into the labyrinths of your soul.

The butterflies of pity
Drift silently
Into a redefinition of the modern mother.

Written in soft Cyrillic lettering your image
—Celestial!—
Turns the world's innocent tears to fresh ink,

---

1. Important Polish poet, living in Ukraine.
2. Vranjska Banja: hot spring baths in Serbia.

Let your pen flow its hope upon
The naked sheets,
To vivify compassion's aquarelles;

Promising how one day *Homo sapiens*
Will recognize
Woman as the life of life itself,

Without whom
Humankind
First would go mad, then fade away to silence.

My Mother's Hand

I read my mother's hand
That my honor higher stand:

All, written in fine lines
That turn to furrowed signs:

Mosaic of uncompliant,
The grieved hand of a saint:

Wharves where the ships of pain
Dock for the night again.

The Highland Singer

Skeined into music the breath of that girl of the
  highlands
Gently wakened the drowsy alpine pastures,

Mingled the breeze of summer with the chill of the
  snow scour,
Cooled with its touch the massive chests of the
  mountains.

Kindly the hills passed on to the valleys those
  pastorals,
Gave us those fresh and delicate shepherd melodies:

Not a drop of morning dew was toppled,
Not a trace of pollen shaken from the flowers,

Cedar by towering cedar, pine by pine
Life-thick root fingers darkly gripping the meadows,

Felt the thrilling milk sap flow through their boles,
And Fragaria flowers turned untimely to
  strawberries.

Mother Teresa

It was so hard
for her life
to close its parentheses.

But still,
between them
she remains
an equation
unsolved to the end.

Gonxhe Bojaxhiu[1]

More silently than poverty itself

she peeled off the skin from her body
to patch the wounds of others.

She gave us everything
when she had nothing to give.

1. Mother Teresa's birth name.

Metaphysics

Truth

Truth
Is an asymptote.

We are the curve of the search.

However hard we try to close on it
Never can we touch it.

Hallelujah

The empty spaces between the letters
of the word *conclusion*
cubicize the silences
in their echoic frames—
invisible lances
like the notes of a late piece of music
after a midnight
with no date in the calendar.

Well-intentioned in content
they invite you to crystallize
but not to petrify.

The philosophy of such occasions
remains a riddle
without a solution.

At last, in the end,
intelligence
unweaves the web of theories
and runs amok with guesses.

But the wisdom of the sages
takes the bottom line of the equals sign,
turns it upright, moves it carefully
toward the center of the unmoved line
and boom!
they have crossed them into a plus.

Their hands a pyramid pointing toward Jupiter.

Hallelujah!

While Seconds Turn to Minutes

While seconds turn to minutes
the twilight vanishes without complaint.
Earth and sky crack like an eggshell
without the usual cramps of a birthing mother.
From its zebra breast it drips
carelessly the philosophy of human judgement.

The universe, puffing out the smoke of its cigarette,
inscribes in the air certain untold truths:

The opaqueness of the transformation of boy to man,
the impossible tangent that touches the curve of resistance
of a girl when she gives herself away,
the elasticity that catapults a man's life essence
into the radioactive fields of feeling,
the epicenter of moral earthquake
when we cast a verdict in a relative case,
the fact that
the axle of the spinning earth
cannot stand vertical for us
in the presence of each other's real values,

are just some of the reasons why
the magnetic pole of human life
never gets far from the fixed pole of rotation.

The Labyrinth of Tang Thought

The overlord of all and the ruler of Paradise
transformed the prophecy of the stars into
    mountains.
That day Shinshi[1] was christened into the city of God.

With its stylus sharpened on the hides of the stars
it inscribed the laws and moral apothegms
that taught humanity the importance of atavistic art.

A tiger and a bear lived in the same cave
and they prayed and prayed to be human beings.
They did not know the world is but a system of
    logarithms.

They had to adapt to the smell of garlic
and to undress the sun with their eyes for a hundred
    days.
And the tiger in rage broke his teeth on his chain.

Only the bear dressed up the cave with walls of
    patience
and after three more weeks turned into a woman
    made of numbers,
unaware that the Roman numbers had no zero.

---

1. In Shinto, Shinshi ("divine messenger") or Kami No Tsu-kai, an animal spirit familiar.

The Spontaneous Energies of Matter

The self-born energies of matter in motion
generate an order that ignites a discharge
sparking mind's advance across its own last border.

Infinity has never been defined;
berserk speculation seeks its own blessing
on the open wings of its untamed dreams.

Nothing can conquer unmeasured space
as long as its dimensions go on swelling
beyond the bleary eyes of whatever century this is.

Cosmic rays collide above in radioactive bursts,
and they are probes to show us what we may
    become
above the death struggle of polarized humanity.

A Journey to the Center of the Self

So if the moral consequence of life is consciousness
and consciousness is not an endless ring, a self-
    closed song,
then let's not beat about the bush, confess:
where in the intricate kingdom of ourselves do we
    belong?

We live within the acrobatics of the blush,
between our ignorance and our shamed nakedness;
we fear what we don't know, but worse, the bitter
    touch
of echoes that we recognize, yesterday's
    unrighteousness.

We search for what we know we are in our
    betrayals,
in those late hours where wishes can't defeat the
    possibilities,
how we ignored that great moral field of gravity in
    which all sails,
invaded to the core of others' feelings, broke their
    boundaries.

Poets

With Neruda on the Atlantic Shore

Each time a poet dies, something dies in me.
thinking of Neruda, I walk to the Atlantic.

Enhanced with the eyes of a blue dragon
and with the greatest sophistication,
the widest open arms,
the most sublime seriousness,
the most inspiring memories inscribed in its waves
the Atlantic riffles the sunny pages of the shores
and the love lyrics of Neruda.

We sit cross-legged by the Atlantic, then rise.
Eye to eye with its endless dazzle,
frowning I mutter something in Albanian
and he, abstracted, murmurs something in
    Oceanian.

At once the waves clash more maturely,
and they take a photo of the poet on the book
    jacket,
and dance about me more delicately
as they archive it in their eyes among their oceanic
    secrets.

As an open champagne bottle boils
the waves spit white foam from their mouths
and mermaids dance about the lyrics of the poet

an old waltz borrowed from the Corybantes
to the music Mozart composed in secret
as an anthem for the true artists of Paradise,
this time for Ricardo Eliécer Neftali Reyes Basoalto,
whom even the Atlantic has accepted as deeper than
    itself.

Florida, September 23, 2003

Snow in Beograd[1]

As if it had erased all its cares in heaven,
ever so calmly the snow covers earth,
cold,
featherlight,
relying on that old-fashioned kind of flight,
never dreaming that upon touching ground
it might be trampled
or melted,
indifferent that its appearance in this world
makes humans gaze with astonishment
at its leisurely fall!
The few who are clad in fur coats
stick out their tongues with hedonistic pleasure,
lovers easily convert it into steam
the second it contacts the hot coals of their lips,
the healthy merely rub their hands
           to warm up a little.
While the others, oh, the others!
They marvel at how the snow descends
           without a whisper of warning!
They wonder how gravity can draw down such
   lightness
but can't find the strength to free it
           from the weight of grief

---

1. Marinaj spent the winter of 1990–91 in Beograd in exile, installing telephone lines.

that long ago once burdened
their innocent souls!

The Poet Frederik Rreshpja[1] Was Born Today

On the day of his death

The poet Frederik Rreshpja was born today, for his life
as we know it, escaped him in a rush.
But it was only his death that dropped to the ground

that it might understand him: it spread two black sheets across his eyes
(which were not looking at anything in particular),
and sprinkled with darkness the earth about him

where he lay, hugged him to its chest,
looked over its shoulder like the thief
who stole a portrait of Rembrandt. Only death, then,

recognized the real essence of the poet.
Laws were and remained on the books. Justice
was and remained in interpretation. His antique griefs

were and remained torches of triumph.
The waves of his poetic rhythms did not react
in accord with the advent of that final sunset.

---

1. Important Albanian poet, imprisoned by the communists for his views, who died in poverty.

The continual metamorphosis of his prophecy at
    long last lost

its absolute control over the poet
and over his epoch
as a man. The crystalline carbonates did not
formulate new theories about the interruption

in the blinking of the poet's eyes—
a black bow tie in an inextricable knot—
terrifying sculptures of faces that
stand projected on the castle walls of Rozafa.[2]

The poet long ago had lost his body's harmony
and his mind's. But as for the coordination of his
    spirit
with his verse—no. All this on the platform
that Lucifer has projected for the Albanian poets.

His adventures in life's tyranny and neglect
became his inspiration, the peace and refuge of his
    soul. In his
consciousness flew an inexplicable intellect:
as his spirit evolved into the company of the dead
    poets.

---

2. Albanian castle with a tragic history. On Rozafa the person, see p. 32n2.

For him his days were inoperable. They were
the internal weaknesses of a renovated man.
It's only today that those exhaling dungeons, his
    lungs,
turned into fairy boats whose sails are trimmed
    toward greatness.

The Poet

Over the white page
His eyes have turned to eyeglasses.

As a proud pencil
Finely sharpened
He keeps going
Until his lead is spent.

Sunday Prayer

> *Father, forgive them; for they know not what they do.*
> —Luke 23:34

On Sunday I prayed for the republic:
for cannibals to sprout claws
         and morph into beasts,
for beasts to become gentle
         and turn into humans,
for humans to grow wings
         and change into angels,
for angels to descend from heaven
         and convert into poets,
for poets to conceive of words
         that blossom into poems,
for poems to transform
         and metamorphose into
Plato's proof of the "objective truth."

Where Can I Find the Spirit of the Poet?

It turned to a heart in my skeleton
(the dead told me)
It turned to a numbness in my pain
(the wounded told me)
It turned to a touch at my departure
(the beautiful one told me)
It turned to the banked embers of my fire
(poetry told me)

Where do I find the spirit of the poet?
His spirit I can never know
But I saw his body thrown down,
impaled in a pit of meat hooks
(said the truth)

The Poets Start Over on Mondays

The week divides poets into seven thin sheets of light.

Monday asks of them the sound of their shoes on the sidewalk;
digests the rhythm of the poet and the rhythm of his poetry.

Tuesday starts drinking from the open bottle that was forgotten,
anxious that the poet's shoes might be wearing thin.

Wednesday scowls like Macbeth
and demands that the poet apologize for entering it at all.

Thursday leaves him a thousand bad messages in his notebook
and tries to isolate him in a bubble.

Friday doesn't even want to know what the poet means;
both Shakespeare and Cervantes died on Friday.

Saturday remains only a weekend day, a poet only a poet,
and the most striking metaphors must wait until Sunday.

Sunday the poets are asked to pay for the sins of the week:
ink jurors in paper courts

condemn them to start from scratch again on Monday.

Homer

Homer decoded
the abstractions
of the old philosophers—

Those trails they blazed
in the Sphinx's pyramids
down to the center of their thought,

the pre-Morse alphabet
inscribed
into the songs of Solomon.

Pure he kept it,
far from the antique misconception
that everything true must be in ink and paper.

He redefined the oral codes,
spun their great bale of wool onto two spindles
between the letter *I* and the number *0*.

Meadow

Slowly the meadow was now licked across
by this long brilliant tongue of light.
The stars bestowed upon the sky a kiss
and vanished from their sight.
The bubbling spring breathed forth a dove
of vapor seeking for its loving sea;
The laurels cursed the pitfalls set for hope and love
in eyes of innocence that weep in misery.
The sun, a lovestruck boy, arose amid its beams,
and set upon each fingered branch a ring of glory,
and my clasped hands became a book of poems
waiting to be opened by girls who want a story.

To the Birds

Only the struggle of the sun's great silences
with the deceitful phantoms of the truth
comfort your last songs of the evening.
Without even touching the grey shades of twilight
you whip off the black cover of the night's cage
and you weave into your nests the evening's blank
  dismay.

Why do you roost so early, my little poets?

Can you no longer endure to look eye to eye
with the disappointment of the day's collapse?
Is that why you go to bed offended and
  heartbroken?
I know. Your songs condemn themselves to those
  closed ears
in the dungeons where my genius fingers digitalize
  for free . . .

But you are not the only ones caged in your aging,
kept from the light waves of your own voice,
you who feel your life is barren,
who stretch your courage out, wait too for the rising
  tempos of the dawn,
as you scratch in zeros and ones your inner griefs,
wind round your necks the innocent scarves of
  mourning.

If ever the musical meadow of your souls caught fire,
that fire would be found transplanted into
    tomorrow,
hidden in the eyes of those of your faith, dear poets,
for birds like poets, poets like birds, must live and
    die.

The Cave Bear in the Trial of Words

The moment they avoided the pitfall set for them
by the heavy cannibalistic paws of the Sankosëve,[1]
words began to transform the foundations of peace.

A pentangle star whose points flamed with reason
murmured something in the ears of the galaxies
about how human sympathy had been broken into
    abstract factions.

They poured their images of hate
into the skull of an ancient *Ursus spelaeus*.[2]
Any unspoken words were crushed as deserving of
    punishment

by an odd combination of enemies—
because words expressed can turn to a golden chain
    of celebration
about the neck of the termite-riddled cross.

The destiny of the poets, who in despair
were composing an anthem for the fallen heroes,
was overruled. They asked no questions, they
    already knew the answers.

---

1. Mythological tribe in north Albanian folklore who trapped wild animals in pitfalls and then led their enemies to fall into them as well, to be devoured by the starving beasts.

2. Latin name for cave bear.

Was it that they lacked personal chemistry with the
 bloody jurors,
rotten as they were? In any case, that didn't help.
Even the termite queen's philosophic metaphors were
 smashed

down to some place beyond the soft neons of human
 compassion,
discarded like the frail snakeskins
left in the pit's piled skulls.

Reason and suffering were buried in soot.
The inner spirit of the people started to explode in
 secret.
The twisting of the words was just a trap set only
 for them,

so their conformity might be worth more than their
 dreams,
and they would know that, just like poets, words
 have necks,
and whether before them or after, can be hanged by
 a rope.

Poetry

Spirit whitens into spirit.
    Every word
strikes miraculous sounds
              from the contact of philosophy
with feeling.

    At just one moment in a day
          a rolling avalanche
furiously scans the human anatomy:
the protesting voices of the bowel,
    the irregular pauses of the heart,
the woodland litter of the human brain.

    It draws itself together
and burns up without ash
    in the poets' eyes:
    salt from the tears of men and gods—
a double handful of fire for the phoenix.

Prose

Lava
    still red in the face
rises up
    surges higher
to the climax, the zenith:
its logic obeys its own laws.

It's not always
    In the first person—
        Its forms more elastic than its matter.

Sparkles of noise
    grind
        like mineral samples in a geologist's bag:
    their friction
    dies out
like vision in a dead man's eyes,

the earned darkness
    the newest riddle
        engraved in Albanian on the gates of Hades.

Where Was I Last Night?

A morning riddle

Where the trees like to murmur
Where the silence wants to sing
Where the flowers love to grow
Where the finch delights to drink

Where the river draws its bow
Where the water ripples rhyme
Where the pens all come to think
Where the moon peeps out at night

Where the shores are metaphors
Where water speaks in metric feet
Where the stars pour out their shine
Where the waves in secret meet

Where God keeps his green eye
Where the river flows and glows
Where poems strike the sky
Where the poet lights the words.

Haiku

Outside the window
the dawn's first light summons us
to blaze up with it.

Earth

The Blue Nile

I am the sacred tear of Ethiopia,
I weep with you, laugh with you forever,
the Blue Nile or the Great Abbai—
I don't care which name you know me by.

I run down from the beautiful eye of Mount Gish.
For you I blaze a landmark in the desolation;
my gurglings have the power of a god;
I place the dot upon the divine *I*.

Adored and hated,
I am the watery signature of Abyssinia,
honored and feared,
I am the pen and the ink of justice.

Ever I flush out from the earth the good soil,
in my belly I raise fish and crocodiles.
Mosquitoes, malaria, and other diseases
I turn into pistils at the center of the life flower.

Many powerful spirits are at my command:
Some are saints, some are demons.
In many lands I am held as if a god;
I am feared even by those who trust me.

Forever I lick thirstily at the volcanic rocks
but I never change the rainy season,

though I am swollen and thickened by the silt
I protect always the alphabet of flotsam on my
 margin.

Fuji

The skeptical part of the philosophy of Fuji-San[1]
is written, erased, and written again
in the roots of its premature gray.

The maps of the functioning brain
at the center of human thought
determine its spiritual dimensions.

Fuji's philosophy denies there is any lack of genetic evidence,
but values as it values itself the essence of unique solitude
because there are no words, only thoughts.

Lake Yamanaka erases the primitive inscriptions
on the lowest stratum of Lake Motosu
both for it and for the citizens of Gotemba.

Everything that imagination can conceive
Fuji thought's magnetic pull turns into life
as an added mineral layer in the bluish waters.

After the recurring clash of the tectonic plates
new chances became the life of the future:
it veiled only the old eyes of Tokyo.

---

1. *San*: Japanese term of respect, applied to persons and certain august objects.

Sokolovac,[1] Summer 1998

The mountains of Iasbina[2]
like girls' unbuttoned bosoms
have donned me like a thin tress of mist.
From up here
where flares the verdant forest of the poet, I see
the realm of Sokolo combing his hair in the mirror
    of the Danube.
The mountains primp themselves—no fear lest their
    shadows
fall across the border of Romania.
That's why the white pigeons,
whiter than the end of the revolution itself,
refuse to sing the old tunes.
Here the ashes of the past
and the pollen of the future
meld to a tenable and indissoluble glass.
Through it all,
that life of the Sokolonians, staunch to the end,
displays itself cleanly and searchingly
like a vivid sign before a yet-to-be-written fate.
They make me braver
to dress the whole place with poetry,
like two pairs of smoldering lips in a lovers' kiss.

1. Serbian spelling of Sokol, a Serbian-speaking town in Romania.
2. Iasbina: beautiful highland region by the Danube in Romania.

But, too, they turn my courage into grief:
from the lap of the mountains I spread my face
as a weeping willow extends its tresses,
to smell the disheveled roses
that still, alas, are rooted in human blood.

So It Seems, at Ha Long Bay[1]

I

Ha Long Bay must have been one of God's
 embryonic creations,
A model for the rest of the natural world to see and
 follow,
A warm magic shell for the earth to incubate its
 core,
Made of sea-like sky and sky-like sea floating in our
 universe.

These tiny islands have distinct souls and are souls
 themselves.
They are poetic compositions and compose poetry of
 their own.

As you dream walk in between their metaphorical
 meadows
They dreamingly rearrange and spell your name:
The rock formation alters its layers into characters
 of your alphabet
and as they gently vibrate the tranquil sea
The smooth waves welcome you in your own
 language.

---

1. The translator, who has been to this beautiful bay in Vietnam, vouches for the accuracy of the poet's hyperbole.

Ha Long Bay whispers benevolently and is human to the core.
Its few villagers are archetypical history and make history.

II

Ha Long Bay is truly natural, yet it appears divine.
Here you do not have to die to receive Paradise:
Simply open your eyes and your whole being feels heaven.

Feel the rhythms of your heartbeat bring back the human being in you
The spine of the growing web of your soul will get you back to the reality.

III

Don't bother.
Trying to recreate Ha Long Bay is like trying to recreate perfection.

Ireland, knowing it deserves consideration as one of the wonders of the world
Tried and had to settle for the Cliffs of Moher.

Gilgamesh, banking on his status of being one of the first poets
Tried and had to settle for his epic.

The whole notion of beauty, at the risk of being
 eternally redefined,
Tried and had to settle for being called "Aesthetics."

The sky, taking advantage of being closest to God
Tried and had to settle for its mysterious stars and
 ever-changing arrangements of clouds.

Solomon, not knowing someday it would be
 published in the Bible
Tried and forgot to mention God in Song of Songs.

God himself, it seems, in creating a second natural
 wonder
Tried and settled for seeing it broken into six other
 pieces alongside Ha Long Bay.

Footprints in Hollywood

Today the afternoon was whispering in my ear
to come out sober from the wedding feast of dreams,
keeping a straight face,
in fitted jeans,
selected words.

Today my voices and my shadow will make love.
Hollywood:
a foggy poem on the face of lunacy:
you're like the way the poet's wrinkles come in
    waves,
you're like the traveling torch of the Olympiads.
Here people come to squeeze another self out of
    themselves
and leave like angels with burnt wings.
You're like a hundred skies just loaded up with
    rainbows.

The platforms of today get slowly lost in the levels of
    the evening
shaken by wings rehearsing for tomorrow on the
    violin.

And then there's the jacarandas.
They appear before me in their thin chemise,
drop on my face a violet plasm of smiles
as I open for them and for myself
the coffin of old desires condemned to be hanged.

Eiffel Tower

Shadowy
creation
of dreams

The pen
of God
out of steel
and shine

Like France

it draws
our fingerprints
upon the cosmos

A paysage
lost
in translation
between earth
and sky.

Abstraction

Fabric
    of the spirit
        torn in the middle—
            life.

    Francisco Goya's
  panel in blood
death in art—

        crime in oils.

India

To Be a Guest in the House of Rita De

The sunflowers turn their backs upon the sun—it's
    true!—
to be the first in greeting you.

The hinges squeak when you come in
to welcome you before the good host can begin.

The sofas hold their breath until you take your
    place,
beating the host's smile in the welcome race.

The food aroma writes in steam a word
a second quicker than the plates can touch the
    board.

The glasses clink each other, cry out "Cheers!,"
    advance,
invite the cutlery to a Bengali dance.

Cuisine and conversation flare up now
before the books of poems can start to glow.

The eyelids close in sweet surrender in between
sheets whose whiteness silences itself unseen.

The Hindu gods that guard the books all day
tonight watch over poets' prayers where they lie.

The morning sun draws back the drapes, comes in
    and beams
while birds make anthems of the words they spoke
    in dreams.

Sugar confides, before it melts in the tea
why "bindi" is the caste mark worn by Mousumi,

why Hestia's[1] more like Atithi Devo Bhava[2]
than Rhea her mother and Cronus her old father.

---

1. Roman goddess of the hearth.
2. Hindu goddess of hospitality.

The Lost Layers of Vyasa's Skin

PART 1

At the Apsaras Aerodrome their midnight eyes were
   waiting for me
   with more welcoming arms than Ganesha;[1]
In the echoes of silence Parvati and Shiva named me
   their son
   —jokes about wealth forbidden!—
Erasing the verbs from all possible sentences
   mentioning
   why fish die faster in the air of Calcutta.

With hearts bigger than their bodies they opened
   their doors to me,
   as if they were old books of treasure;
I stood before them like the space between two
   prohibited words,
   mouth open like two currentless cables,
A limp tongue that could not taste the breast milk of
   Annapurna,
   with a language whose lexicon lacked the word
   for Babel.

My thoughts dissolved like ink in holy water,
   parched, I thirsted for the River Ganges,

---

1. Elephant-headed Hindu god of prosperity.

To flow in the delta of purification and pardon,
>   lost between painter and philosopher:
My lips the parched lips of human liberation and global disaster,
>   mumbling the lyrics of an unknown love song.

How could I know that India is its own unbordered Laccadive,
>   a peaceful catalyst in the permutation of the core ideas,
A fount of civilization, erasing any thought of separate oceans,
>   that gathers all waters, one forever and not five,
Epicenter of light rays, equidistant, burning away any injustice
>   to those souls who feed only on human love.

And my being begins to transform like a photo in the developer,
>   I melt, cave in to this newest rift, and begin to sound India
As the tectonic plates part and the fault lines open;
>   knowing the further I enter, the harder it is to return,
Like Mother Teresa who went so far in she never came back,
>   the trail from human to saint in a cloud of unknowing.

PART 2

But I shall trail her into this holy land's deep mystery,
>seeking to solve our chaotic paradoxes
As if we were two dreamers tuning in to the same heavenly melody
>with faces whose set grimace is a map in human flesh
Of that imaginary alien path, a myth detached from faith,
>above and beneath the bed of the restless sea.

As if I had learned nothing from Narmer's Victory Palette
>I'll ask Indra, my Indo-European cousin
For a passport to the hearth of Vedavati's[2] fire
>and pledge to adhere to the rites of protection
For the tenets of cryptic knowledge, swift access
>To the logic of orphans, the crippled, and the poor.

The inner barriers of honest folk must be set by,
>the afterdeath of troubled souls redefined.
I'll morph myself into the axles of the sky wagons,
>nor doubt what strictures of the ancient magic
I meet on my search for a new path through India's past
>lit by the lightnings of the frowning sky.

---

2. Vedavati: Hindu goddess of prosperity, avatar of Lakshmi.

I'll be the dilemma that bears on its shoulder the
　　chill of delay,
　　　　an avatar calling the horns of Kanglasha[3] to
　　ward off the devil,
a wishbone of two new credos, unbroken, and with
　　no inequality,
　　　　bridging the shattered world into one clean hand.
May my spirit be not of the hanging tree but of the
　　dancing tree:
　　　　lit with the glamor of passage, of fall, of fate.

As a stranger at dawn, blessed by Varuna[4] and
　　Mitra,[5]
　　　　Ahalya[6] will melt me under her tongue
And lay me on the lunar course through the
　　underworld
　　　　to create a new dispensation:
Mitra will lend me his rays to raise up a new cosmic
　　race
　　　　rewrite the compact of nature with its new
　　human nation.

Varuna serenely will tear off a strip of her silken
　　gold dress.
　　　　I'll write an oath on its parallel patterns:

---

3. Kanglasha: lion-like dragon deity.
4. Varuna: god of the sea.
5. Mitra: god of treaties.
6. Ahalya: goddess of beauty.

In a stone-textured alphabet stemming from two
> gods and a poet,
> > to layer a cast for a broken peace,
And we'll inscribe "get well soon" on the Hindu
> pantheon
> > with sharp chisels made of the bones of mortal
> > anguish.

I will keep Durga's[7] unruly lion locked in my rib cage,
> and leash the fierce god's tiger to my neck;
And I'll pick out for her at random two more human
> arms,
> > put paper in one hand, a pen in the other.
Since India's final history never was written, its
> people unstudied,
> > Mahishasura[8] can be defeated only with paper
> > and ink.

PART 3

For this I shall build a monastery in my chest
> and be an anchorite,
Resume that ascetic math
> that does not deal with numbers,
Become an echo that repeats
> the sobs and tears of mortal plight,

---

7. Durga: fierce many-armed mother goddess.
8. Mahishasura: half-human, half-buffalo demon.

Fill in the intimate detail of human endurance
    in the war with crime; learn
To conduct with tenderness those silent melodies
    that blush to hear themselves,
The hopes that snake through the gorges
    of a fate that has forgotten to return.

May I fall in love with Parvati,[9]
    she of the wonder beyond the darkness,
That she be appointed the goddess
    of my weaknesses and strengths,
In merciless war with the demons
    of that very darkness.

I'll light no candles for human sacrifice;
    pour poetry's oil on the flames, and sing.
I'll bow down with the settings of the suns
    that burn themselves to make the light.
Exhausted then I'll challenge
    the anti-gods of the anti-folk of the antiquity of suffering.

When I have embraced that Chhavapal,[10]
    the crone that life had reduced to a fist,

---

9. Parvati: goddess of energy, harmony, and love; wife of Shiva.

10. Chhavapal: Bengali mythological figure who can shrink herself in size.

Who pours her rage out at this life
    by twisting clay into vessels,
Mud as warm as the guts spilled
    from a black ram flayed alive in August,

We'll call on the address in the Upanishads
    where the wise Yajnavalkya[11] dwells
To debate with him the cruxes
    of Indian physics and metaphysics,
Compose together a new treatise
    on human goods and ills,

Like Sri Gopal Paul[12] who with his seven *Ampans*[13]
    makes, each year, from a mess
Of hay and wire and mud
    Gods and goddesses renewed,
Sculptures that perfect the images of deities
    and the worshippers they bless;

As for the consciousness and misbehavior
    of our euphoric century as a whole,
Without in any way dismissing
    the epistemology of Neti-Neti,[14]

---

11. Yajnavalkya: Hindu sage, philosopher, and mediator.
12. Sri Gopal Paul: Indian artist who creates sculptures of the gods out of mud, straw, and wire.
13. Assistants.
14. In the Upanishads, neither this nor that.

It is necessary that we discover the universality
    of the principle of Atman, of the soul:

Take, for example, that deaf-mute boy
    Subit Kundu[15] the embroiderer,
Who sews with pearls forbidden dreams
    upon the hems of wedding dresses,
Making with fingers cunning in their art
    the meadows of the soul yet lovelier;

Did Yainavalkya's theory upon
    the necessary disconnection from the world of time
Originate before or after his famed dialogue
    with Gargi Vachaknavi and Maitreya,[16]
And is not calling self a mere play of phenomena
    a code that might become a crime?

PART 4

Kneaded with sweat the swollen dust becomes
    a perfect clay to fashion into art;
The muddy hands of folk whose spirit is white gold
    have lost their fingernails in it;

---

15. Contemporary deaf-mute artist in Manta, near Kolkata.
16. Gargi Vachaknavi and Maitreya: ancient philosophers of truth-telling.

And thus they turn my chest into a castle and
    to a sculpture shaped like India, my heart.

Each step I take becomes a link invisible
    within a chain of thirst and sorrow,
Each heartbeat digs foundations
    in which my feet are deeply foundering,
Each breath archives in my spirit
    thousands of faces gazing at a far tomorrow.

I dwell, a poet, in the labyrinth
    of all their human loves and agonies,
Where every form of love has come
    to cheer me on my coming passage;
As if they've turned me to a hive where life
    can hum its secrets without fear, they come like bees.

Is a true life philosophy the magic of the myths
    or the reality of civic being, or some other thing?—
What is it that inspires me thus to stay in India
    or carry India with me wherever I may go?
Why does it feel so natural
    to love a people of such bravery and suffering?

In Amta then where muddy sidewalks grab by the throat
    Life's archetypal tones and tints

I entered in the precinct of Lord Shiva's[17] temple,
   prayed for the art of true telepathy;
And now its colors glow, a loving heart shape forms
   out of the twined trunks of two elephants,

Shiva the dancing god of making and unmaking
   spread his four arms in hospitality.
We set the rules of this my expedition, the ordeals
   I must meet so I discover India;
He opened his third eye, destroyed my physicality,
   and in a mystic form he recreated me.

First he allowed me to retain those true and fiery feelings
   of love and of respect for this great land,
Permitted me the readiness to sacrifice it all
   to enter in the nature of its people,
That I may study strategies of wise resistance
   against betrayal's cruel hand.

He gave me a slab of glistening mica and spoke:
   This is of nature but not just a mineral,
It will serve your quest and serve the needs of humanity,
   It is a natural guide but not a topography,

---

17. Shiva: god of creation and destruction, member of the supreme trinity of Brahma, Vishnu, and Shiva.

A sacred secret awaiting its resting-place, but not a
    novelty,
        It doesn't need you, but your life depends on its
            miracle.

He said I'd face surprises, pain, and challenge
    (less than the Indians' own, let it be said);
That real and fantastical will often switch
    and take each other's place without a warning,
That I may choose four helpers on the way
    but that their powers will be limited.

So Doctor Hsemar, healer, philosopher, and poet,
    I shall bring with me:
Sophist by day, at night a mole
    who digs the tunnels of all literature,
My language mentor and interpreter
    among the savage monsters of the sea;

And Atibas, writer, Sophist within his soul,
    and advocate for all the trials of youth,
Equilibrist of justice's mercuric scale,
    judicious prescriber of euphoria,
Shall in the accusing courts of the underworld
    stand by me as the voice of reason's truth;

Atir, a queen of poets, teacher, speaker
    for every Indian protonist,
Switchboard of telepathic commerce
    between the living and the gods,

In duels with the ruthless sorceresses there,
    shall act as my spiritual strategist;

Imusuom, professor, editor, translator,
    and mute voice for all the human silences,
A rare bilingual book that can't be understood
    by a first reading, still less by its cover,
Will counsel me upon discretion in my words
    when provocation tempts me to excess.

PART 5

Now I find myself alone in a lifeless region
    deep in the Bay of Bengal.
Here on the seabed there's nothing but heaps
    of grotesque and skeletal fish bones
On a seafloor goosebumped with terror
    under a changeless pall.

In despair this desert, abyssal, has wept from itself
    all of its oxygen long before,
Anaerobic biota that grab up the nitrogen
    since have invaded this ghastly fossil realm.
And I, the stranger, am suddenly wrapped in a maelstrom
    foaming with madness. I am its core.

I cannot peel out my body's own bundle of nitrogen
    that might give life to even one dream,

There isn't a chance I can save the last traces of oxygen
    evaporating off in the distance;
Impotent here to balance the nutrients matching the measure
    of life in this ocean regime.

In this tropic sterility now the maelstrom, sick of pollution,
    convulses into a different state:
Struggling with human corruption
    It buds off a new maelstrom in me
That rages, starving, anoxic, across these death zones
    and suddenly opens the way to a gate.

Marked on its portals in images lie
    open green paddy fields, a noble mountain chain;
Nothing could be more vivid than, look!,
    the tones of the colors,
Waves of light that stir my nerves
    and speed up the light of my brain.

And Soma came to me, leafed in the shape of a narcotic,
    Soma, the god of inspiration,
And so released me from suffering, taught me
    the six priorities of life beyond the gate,
Clothed me in a lucent shift, that in any dark would glow
    writ with a text, *Moksha*, illumination:

The word that taught me the cycle of death and
   rebirth
   and freedom from samsara, from all illusion,
Acquainting me with my own new form
   of liberty and enlightenment,
Empowered by gnosis, released from ignorance,
   guarded from any delusion.

PART 6

As a being advised and guarded
   by such piety as befits a mortal,
Anxious about which way
   the clock hand is turning,
I followed the urge that took me
   to pass alone through the shining portal.

And I walked through an array of trajectories
   whose invisible target was not evident;
I paralleled the trail of bubbles
   left by the footsteps of Mother Teresa,
To find how India had given her the means
   to blaze her trail from nun to saint.

On the far side of the gate the silence bit its lips
   and kept all things suspended. No advice.
But now the thunder crashed and clap on clap
   in Morse code beat out its message to me:

Will you pay your passage
>   in money, information, ideas, or sacrifice?

I ask where are the four counselors
>   Lord Shiva had permitted me?
Good money, key information, a big idea—
>   or do you want a sacrifice?
What kind of currency do you accept? How much
>   do I need?
>   How do I earn the fee?

To solve the riddle of the currency—
>   your survival hinges on the same—
Remember the highlands in the book
>   your mentor Renrut Derf once recommended,
And the shining of a fish that is prejudged
>   in value and in name.

The message turned the turbine of my memory
>   to readings offered by my counselor
Hsemar, who, constrained to speak in numbers only,
>   Uttered, "1816."
And Atir spoke, but she could only say
>   that I must not think "Highlands" meant Malësia.

The introduction to the *Popular Tales*
>   *of the West Highlands* came to me
And the name of Hector Urquhart
>   and his wise words

That one man's trash can be another's treasure
    woke in my memory.

So what the thunder spoke of was that fish
    so hard to clean it cheats the fisher's knife:
The rough fish, trash fish,
    the silver carp of Texas:
It was the scales of that despised fish
    that now would save my life.

For such scales I had tracked the smoky spirits
    that migrate only in the night. Now we begin.
We pass through narrow channels
    of dark water in a ferryboat of hope
Whose ribs are our own ribs
    and whose hulls our very skin.

In shallow waters, dark and murky, rough fish swim,
    half death, half dream,
Glowing the water with their soft shine
    following their own destiny;
I didn't have the heart to slay them for their scales
    and serve my self-esteem.

PART 7

Exhausted, I returned to those closed gates
    that held me back from rising higher;

The ocean thunders weighed more heavily upon me,
  told me the choice of money now is lost:
All I had left was one idea, one piece of information,
  or one sacrifice for my desire.

My spirit here was brief and fragile and could break
  in this strange journey under sea,
Denied permission to repeat a trial, denied
  any immunity before the statutes of this realm,
I thought to sacrifice my gift of visionary dream,
  and dreams I know to be the breath of poetry.

The thunders warned me I had left
  but one idea or one key piece of information,
Left me no time to make complaint that I had only
  one chance each
  before the choices disappeared.
The limits of this place had made my freedom
  more horrifying here than in the lifeless zone of
  total isolation.

Suddenly one of Mother Teresa's bubble footsteps
  burst,
  followed by the voices of my guides,
And from the bubble rose a message written in the
  substance
  of an evanescent veil of seaweed strands
Embroidered with blue sequences of illusion
  enveloping my face in gentle tides.

Atir explained it as a tool that would protect me
>   from excesses of sorrow or of joy.
Imousum and Atibas shook their heads,
>   thinking it a weapon against the demons of the sea.
Hsemar insisted this fabric served as a disguise
>   against all dangers,
>   to be used but once before its powers would die.

Confined on all sides by thin crystal walls,
>   I must go only forward, till
I had returned into the sunlit zone
>   where I'd be judged, whether to be turned back
>   or go on;
And at length I found myself beside a giant brain coral,
>   not named a courtroom but the Sea-Life Coral Miracle.

The coral's wrinkled cortex, sectored into living regions,
>   acted what it resembled, a true brain.
"Stand forth and answer truly what we ask:
>   do not be influenced by instinct or persuasion:
If you reason that it is reasonable to reason out your reasons
>   for your presence, begin now to explain."

"Some of the most enlightened minds in India,
>   poets and philosophers, invited me to come for contemplation;

With others, most distinguished poets and
    philosophers in all the world,
    we came to Calcutta just for this;
For we were called for help in this great crisis of the
    planet,
    and to assist in human liberation."

"Irrelevant to the question! Since you didn't listen,
    now you must lose one of your powers: hearing."
"Objection! Nihilism!" interrupted Atibas. "It is his
    first time in India
    and beneath the ocean. He doesn't know the
    rules."
Now the coral changed its messages from voice
    to symbols sparked by sperm and eggs in
    pairing.

"He has talent, education, reputation. The Sea-Life
    Coral Miracle
    will tolerate no ignorance, reason's taint.
If you reason that it is reasonable to reason out your
    reasons
    for your presence, prepare to reason now."
"I come in the footsteps of Nënë Tereza[18]
    to find how India stalled her, guided her from
    nun to saint."

---

18. Albanian name of Mother Teresa. Mother Teresa was born in Macedonia to Albanian parents, and is a saint not only for Catholic Albanians.

"Why do you think the trail of Nënë Tereza
 leads through the depths of the Indian Ocean?
Why do you think her the truest way for you
 into the bone marrow of the spirit of India?
Why do you and your poets believe that such
 impossibilities
 can, when you take them on, be done?"

"Because the marine world's hurt so badly no true
 saint
 can rise to heaven without beginning there.
Because Nënë Tereza is my blood, she speaks my
 language,
 and she's the only saint I've personally known.
Because poets are the most impossible of all of
 nature's works,
 yet give themselves as possible for humankind
 to bear."

"And last: who and what is our common
 danger—
 for the undersea world and all earth dwellers
 that there be?"
"People. The fact that still in all ways big fish eat
 the small,
 with us as it is with you."
"Good luck with your next impossibilities. The Sea-
 Life Coral Miracle
 gives you the title of Citizen of the Sea."

PART 8

I'm free, it seems; but what do I do with this freedom
    here in these alternate spaces where I remain?
I yearn to pass through the zone of darkness, but dare not
    damage my commerce with my conscious self.
A school of graceful dolphins surrounds me,
    directing me gently east to another domain.

It seems an aquademy here where we come to a halt,
    whose students are angelfish girls;
To judge by their conduct, knowledge,
    learned and taught, clearly flourishes;
But something plays with my being, and tampers
    with how my eyes move; my vision whirls.

Imousum comes to me swiftly and measures the pulse
    of my internal peace, disturbed by my changed disposition;
Atir, forgetting my sacrificed hearing, bursts out aloud
    that any delay will be punished by death,
Hsemar signs with his hands that we must act quickly
    for the dreams we deny are the oxygen of a poet's cognition.

I am mesmerized by the colors of the fishes' magical
    faces;
    I lose all self-command in me;
Their talent, elegance, intelligence dissolve me
    like aspirin in tea.
The crystal auditorium turns to a world of its own
    where I become a map of all humanity.

But former zones' punishments do not apply
    in this dark zone, so now I can hear again.
A blue-faced angelfish asks me a question:
    "Do you feel more power to tell or to make the
    future?"
A sea pen asks: "Would you rather be found
    innocent
    when you are accused, or when you're the
    accuser?"

I speak: "Poets project the future on sound
    foundations of thought
    and sculptured façades of words from poetry's
    muse.
A righteous accusation is a self-punishment;
    an unrighteous one is a crime against both
    accuser and accused.
So I feel closer to prophecy than to building a future,
    and desire to be innocent when I accuse."

I feel a red burning in my eyes, even here in the water
    my eyes are dry and out of control;

Hsemar extracts from his pouch a woody paste
  of sandal, and salves my sore eyes,
Saying some words in Bangla that I cannot
  understand,
    their rhythm my comfort, my vision is whole.

Relations between species here at their source are
  balanced
    and filtered, no quarrel of brother with brother.
Here when a creature practices hostile detraction
  it loses forever its undersea inborn immunity;
Every harm has a cost that the damager's paid already,
  so critical vengeance piles one harm on another.

Trade here knows no winter losses, for the
  merchandise
    knows its own value unaided,
A false trader's skill is not in the money cost of his
  ware
    but the buyer's need, and thus he can price it
    unjustly,
But here such merchandise, in its own nature,
  refuses so to be traded.

PART 9

I continue toward a gorge in the greatest depths of
  the darkness,
    where the wonders find their ultimate foundation.

From the first cleft I encounter bursts a new bubble
>speaking in light
>>these words: "Gold in gold and bone in bone."
I must glide like a blind man, rely on my ears to
>avoid the hazards
>>of this strange search for drowned treasures, this
>>dark expedition.

To judge the timing and vectors of sound waves, the
>dolphins
>>had taught me their arts of echolocation.
They may not come any deeper, but thanks to them
>I can learn to deploy other senses than seeing,
And now in my new form my lungs can endure
>liquid oxygen,
>>hold up against the monstrous pressurization.

I have scribed upon sheets of mica
>the counsels of my friends who could not come
>with me,
They are of Nellore muscovite,[19]
>very thin, large, and flexible:
The information there can save my life,
>but their weight's a danger to me in the sea.

I seek the spur of Indian scholars devoted to the
>secrets
>>of the earthly and the oceanic deep,

---

19. A layered transparent mica mined in Nellore, India.

And those Bengali artists who with their works
    have kept alive the ecosystem of the land,
But swimming numbs me in this dark and narrow
gorge
    wherein no trace of solar energy can creep.

The shocking cold now mounts as I go deeper,
    but now I'm tracked by beasts I haven't seen
before.
Strange devil scorpions, skinned like the ocean
floor,
    take me now to their breasts to keep me warm;
I spend the night within the body of a tube-like fish
    that holds me safe in its interior.

The notes inscribed upon my mica sheets with their
advice
    protect me in this world of the unexpected;
Sometimes I must wait hours, masked by the weeds,
    protected by white octopi;
My mentor Renrut has contrived to send my book
    a phosphoric message, by which I am directed:

"Have courage, student mine. Vishnu has held back
    a part of solar energy to shine for you in your
distress.
He has renewed the old core of the cosmic edifice of
laws
    to reconcile the dwellers of the sea with
humankind."

Courage—I seek a courage that is inconceivable, for it maintains
> the possibility of things beyond all human consciousness.

I come into an open space where the path I take branches into three ways: of these
In my mica book I read: the left one leads to magic, the center leads to peace,
> and the right one leads to danger.
Having known magic and danger, and with no other guide,
> I choose to take the way of peace.

The water's getting warmer, quieter now, it loses its viscosity,
> the sea beasts disappear, save only I.
No longer buoyant in this volatile new element,
> my mica block is almost too hard to bear.
Perhaps it is a trap to make me leave my notes behind,
> so I will keep them: together we will live or die.

The mica book's as wide as is my span, as tall as from my knees
> up to my neck, so heavy I can scarcely bear it,
All through my journey it has supported me, but now
> it is a burden to my mind and my attention;

But if my eyes do not deceive me I can see
    a bow tie of light with a translucent shade
    before it.

Gathering myself I surge toward it. Now the water
    gives way to a deep abyss of steam. I fall free.
Gripping my book I pass through levels graced with
    works of art
    fashioned in bone and gold,
Until a thousand hands of light receive me, catch me,
    and in a yellow silken pagri they deposit me.

Is it that now my body is so small,
    or that the silken cap's so large it only seems?
Clearly for the first time I can see my own form
    and the Sanskrit title of my book.
This whole space appears as a botanic garden, one
    whose flora
    is art that's chiseled out of crystal dreams.

My new form is an unfinished sentence in cuneiform
    rising from an ancient tablet like a dust,
And the title of my mica book, scratched there by
    the fingernails
    of readers, is *The Lost Layers of Vyasa's*[20] *Skin*.

---

20. Ancient sage who collected the Upanishads, the early Vedic scriptures.

The silence thunders in me, for whether this place
    is one of magic, danger, or of peace I dare not
    take on trust.

PART 10

From the cliffs of apophyllite crystal on my left
    detaches toward me
    a glittering symbol elaborated from the letter O;
The silence is broken now by its elegant dance,
    but not one of its peach-colored sprays is harmed;
It halts before me and starts to rotate the pagri in
    which I am sitting,
    signs me to come to it, beckons me to reveal:

"How did you come yet alive from the face of the
    earth,
    here to the aquaversity of space comprehension?"
"With the help of sea beasts and friends and the gods,
    Your Excellency, many things become possible."
"So your poet's spirit, our secret gravitic powers,
    and your mica book are not worth a mention?"

"If anything's important, it is worth mentioning;
    since poets,
    even if speaking only for themselves, speak for
    others too;
I find myself here where my mind is sprinkled with
    dew

from the far side of the blessed highlands of the imagination.
In poets' eyes magic and reality are but two lovers who shower together,
for both in their own way are true.

"I see here no human forms, nor yet any sign of aquatic intelligences,
so who are the students here in your aquaversity?"
"For us the planets themselves are as human bodies, consisting of countless molecules, but working as one.
We teach the planets, that they may teach their own dwellers,
each according to its own capacity.

"Come, we must place *The Lost Layers of Vyasa's Skin*
in the treasure house of the faculty of philosophy."
"I cannot now deliver the book to you; it is the only compass I have
to guide me here in this strangest of journeys."
"Without those sheets, Prasthanatrayi[21] cannot be completed:

---

21. The hypothetical complete collection of the 356 Upanishads. Only 108 are known.

That is why Hsemar trusted you to bring them
to me."

We enter an octagon, a space whose walls
    are dressed in black Indian salt,
Adorned with translucent cubes and signs and riddles
    that cannot be solved without breaking them:
The images they form in four dimensions raise in me
    a sharpened turbulence of feeling, with a painful
    jolt.

"Truly you seem too spent to carry on.
    Give me the book and rest here till you're
    stronger."
"I cannot give it till I speak with Hsemar,
    for I still feel as if I struggle with a spell."
"You took the branch of peace—and you chose well
    there at the triple crossroads—no magic is there
    here, nor danger.

"Keep the book, then, till Hsemar and your other
    counselors arrive.
    But now you must rest here a few priorities."
"Priorities? Is there a place where poets can draw
    open
    the drapes of spirit with their cares and limits?
I've sacrificed my gift of dreaming while asleep, but
    poets, to survive,
    can still create their own dreams out of
    virtualities."

"You are confused. For us the word *priority* denotes a stretch of time
 ascending up a pole with zero as its point of origin.
Priorities increase or fall upon this standing line,
 changing according to the greatness of the need.
Come let me take you to the Eye of the Sea
 where in all past priorities all see themselves within.

There you will heal and may now meditate
 upon your definition of the concept, space."
"Defining space? Space is too large and too mysterious.
 How could it be defined?"
"To enter, by tradition, you must give your definition, to be written
 in the black salt walls of this place."

PART 11

And so I'm come to the Eye of the Sea. What's drowned here first
 are pain, fatigue, and sleeplessness.
The Eye is a gigantic teardrop that has paused in its fall
 down the diamond cliff face of the world.
Figured beside its right are six sea-green pupils
 encircled by their dream-tinted multipigmented irises.

And these are spiritual symbols, natural agencies
    as ever imaged by the ancient artists of old India,
Metaphors of the Kolkata poets, melting and
    coalescing
    as mosaics shining in a waterfall,
Flowing unceasing and unhushed
    into the bottomless waters of their idea.

Beyond words mesmerized I sit upon a hassock of
    pure gold,
    one of a row of what seem perfect teeth that
    guard
the ocean's eye, set in a field of beryl aquamarine
    lined with amethyst and tourmaline.
At once a ray of light, glittering with tiny bluish
    motes
    of bentonite swings through—I seize it hard

And pull, and now with every tug the teardrop swells,
    distends to manifest a further vision,
Visions that are no illusion but real happenings
    from various moments of Earth's history;
As soon as each appears, it's cancelled by the image
    of myself still clinging to my mica-block
    commission.

But I am not offended, for I believe in peace
    as much as the challenges it takes to live it;
Were I perhaps to surrender my book to the glyph
    of the letter O, might I be given the full view?

I yearn to know the secrets: will I know the minds
    behind the glyphs,
        the bioluminescent mechanisms, if I give it?

But I have been distracted from the six dream-tinted
    irises,
        focused upon the ocean's eye in all its power;
I see now they reflect, half real, the images
    of my five days of friendship in the terrene world
    above.
Curious, I press toward those sea-green pupils,
    that open to me like a sweet magnolia flower.

In the first pupil there appears a café made of paper
    inked in delicate shades with every form of
    imagery;
Within it boils a human life and harmony
    as natural as the glimmering foam upon the
    coffee:
Alimrahs, Lapog, Ihsrojar, and I
    toast to a better human world with cups of
    poetry.

We speak our lines in lowered voices with that
    melancholy music
        trembling the paper walls of our sojourn,
Our drinks are sweetened with our memories of
    ancient poets
        and philosophers; we bow before their works
        and thoughts.

We etch the date of that cold January in the ribs
    of that dear moment never to return.

The old books, saved in their archival stone, and jacketed
    in hide of crocodiles, serve us as a foundation,
Invite us to look further than the world's prosaic fears
    of the unknown, of the unfashionable,
And use our authorship to fence and guard
    all the downtrodden of each nation.

They beg us to be clear, and tell us that
    the present is the best tense for the verb "to do,"
That love is the debt we owe our planet,
    that must be paid before we enter paradise,
That Buddhi and Siddhi[22] did indeed bless Ganesha
    to take rich Riddhi for his third wife too.

In the second pupil now I see myself about to fall
    in love with a strange sea-maid, no myth to me
Though she's half human and half betta fish,
    for she is more than beautiful, with black-gold scales,
And she has voyaged far through Asian waters
    to coyly test my loving constancy.

---

22. Buddhi and Siddhi: goddesses of intellect and spiritual power, consorts of Ganesha; Riddhi, goddess of wealth, was Ganesha's third wife.

A lovely sweetheart has my heart already,
    and how could I destroy the splendor of that
    love,
But this sea-beauty, more than a mermaid, has the
    power
    to shake this traveler to his very core,
Though yet I know that such great magic in a face
    has often ruined the mortal that it drove.

Unable now to meet with Vätsyäyana,[23] philosopher
    of flesh,
    for he is seven zones of ocean far away,
I shuffle in my mind his Kama Sutra[24]
    that I might so compose my mind in my defense:
Learn that life's strangest miracles can come when
    we resist
    temptation, and work a magic greater than
    magic may.

But the dreamlike mermaid felt my weaknesses;
    as if all human, took me suddenly in her
    arms—
"So thus together we will make a pattern of new
    beauty
    the world has never seen," she whispered in my
    ear.

---

23. Vätsyäyana: Hindu philosopher of sex.
24. The Kama Sutra is an ancient Indian Sanskrit text on sexuality, eroticism, and emotional fulfillment in life.

Almost I fell, but now I cast that tenuous algae veil I had been given
    about me as a camouflage and guard against all harms.

As she left she spoke: "There was no need to guard your honor from me,
    for Vätsyäyana never has defeated me.
But you did well to use your algae veil so to defend your love
    for your own beautiful Atisud,
For I am Maya, veil of illusion, that warps the human sense
    into materialism, and wears down all morality."

In the third pupil is displayed a wonder:
    a divine poet, an Indian philosopher, faints away—
Her eyes fade like the flame in a glass lantern
    that now has spent its final drop of oil—
How is it possible her mighty mind
    Can't keep her standing, make the flesh obey?

In the great hall all eyes and ears
    heedless were focused on the fine oration:
But I'd been drawn in admiration to the faces of the hearers
    and so my eyes were halted on her face.
She needed care more than the lecturer
    there at the podium required my attention.

I started quickly with more hope than expertise
    to keep her in the land of live humanity:
I gave my lungs' air and my soul's love
    until her heart renewed its gentle beat,
My face the first she saw after that sudden breakage
    from the world,
    and somehow she found strength to smile at me.

That smile then was the meaning of my trek to
    India,
    as poet and a thinker of the day:
Her sweet heartbeat so altered the philosopher in me
    that I tore up the speech I'd labored over:
The greatest help the world needs is to those closest
    to us
    and next to others further from our way.

If then the Hindu gods had brought me here to save
    a life,
    one human cell of vital human consequence,
My mission was accomplished—not with my pen,
    that I had given up—but by the real breath of my
    lungs:
Sometimes it's enough that a man be just a man,
    for each saved life is hope for generations hence.

In the fourth pupil I found myself in Howrah,
    a textile factory called Ambika Textile Mills.
I'm with the leader of the union,
    crossing the factory floor in noise and dust;

I exchanged glances with the workers there
    as if we knew each other, and our ills.

But the long tracks of their experience bore a strange idea,
    key to their spiritual world:
Poverty and wealth are but two extremes of heat and cold
    that burn alike, although in different forms,
Or Devas and Asuras[25] who are gods and demons both,
    in endless power struggle whirled.

They don't resent the Rakshas even when they work black magic
    and rack them when their trial's most onerous,
For in their waves of rational will they recognize
    reality both physical and moral,
As light in the Bhabha stairs[26] cascades
    from the collision of the minus and the plus.

In the fifth pupil I'm in a city, crowded as a cricket stadium
    where fans stand closely packed,

---

25. Devas and Asuras: benevolent and malevolent gods.
26. Homi Jehangir Bhabha perfected the mathematics of cascades, which can explain nuclear chain reactions, cosmic ray collisions, and here, by extension, the effect of economic changes.

I'm four floors up, above the hurly-burly
    that seems to keep the sun so dim and distant;
Humbly I enter a Taj Mahal not of white marble but
    of books
    tattered with use, serried and stacked.

This is a real palace of beauty, for even its innards,
    what is between
    its thousands of covers, each is a palace of its own:
All the old and new testaments of Indian and world
    literature
    that are the groaning epicenter of life.
Among these divine glaciers of knowledge and
    mystery
    dwells modestly an eternal Ulysses alone.

He is a golden statue that folk ever carry in their arms,
    the resident deity of the place,
A bust that never changes shirts and does not shave,
    or cry, or suffer praise, or age, or die;
His faithful four floors down call him "our life
    leader":
    Healer Mukhopa, their living grace.

The reason why his name is so hard to remember—
    his only weakness—is a secret that they keep.
He can live days without food, weeks without
    washing,
    months without shaving, years without
    recognition.

He's happy with a boiled potato, a glass of milk, a
    handful of rice;
    A fearless skeptic of pandemics, four floors deep.

They hide that he can't live without his work
    of service to the culture, literature, God, and
    human beings.
He's noted for self-confidence, and for his irony
    toward all metaphysics, and the clock
    measurement of Time,
And to his people he's the Brahma of the spirit,
    of that reality that undergirds all sensory things.

Jaw dropped I wander, one book mountain to
    another,
    drowned in high waves of sheer curiosity
(Too small a being for Healer Mukhopa to see me
    clearly
    but he knows me to be a friend to his own
    kingdom)
Wonder how Brahma came from the golden egg,
    spawned by the chaos waters,
    to bring me home from that immensity.

PART 12

Hsemar—for it is he—lays his hand on my shoulder,
    and around me stand Atibas, Imousum, and Atir.
"What are these thoughts, these deeply unfocused
    glances?"

It is Atir who speaks, and from how they look at
me
I see that none of them saw or knew of the visions
I saw in the pupils that ringed the great tear.

They have come only to urge me to surrender
the muscovite book, and soon are gone.
The glyph called "O" signals to me to go back
to the octagon where I had entered.
I give her the book. She opens it, sets it upon the
shrine,
and now it merges, becomes one with the stone.

She bids me walk on her left deeper into the
octagon
till the light at the entrance has faded away
Into darkness lit by two sources only:
an external force and internal energy field.
"Form with your hands a pyramid before you:
give voice to both energies," softly I hear her say.

At once I remember Renrut, my mentor, his
phosphoric message,
and the demanded definition of space; aroused
within,
I beg Vishnu for his gift of that moiety of the sun's
energy
that he had saved for me to give me light,
And humbly offer my mother's definition:
space is an open organism of organic origin.

For a moment I heard only my words echoing
 around the corners of the octagon till they
 returned to me;
When suddenly a beam of light extended, followed
 the journey of my voice about the octagon,
And then rebounded to the far wall where this text
 was waiting:
 "Epicenter of the Power of Zero: The
 Interplanetary Aquademy."

Now beneath this title the bright ray encoded and
 engraved:
 "Space is an open organism of organic origin."
Then the whole octagon lit up with two green suns
 orbiting each other high on the far wall
And I am perched upon a pedestal held up
 by four rough fish fossilized to stone.

O spoke, and told me I must introduce myself
 and make petition to the lords of the aquademy.
"Aquajeta![27] Greetings! I feel as if I were an alphabet
 scribed by a seagull upon the face of the Indian
 Ocean,
A primal cell of an ecosystem, roaming the shores,
 dreaming of giving birth to the science of
 biology.

---

27. Aquajeta: a neologism in Albanian, meaning "water of life."

"My wish is my mission: to meet with Saint Teresa
    to learn the secrets of the Indic civilization."
"You brought the book. Thanks be to you and to
    your counselors.
    Prasthanatrayi[28] is complete.
And for your sacrifice we will immortalize your
    definition
    Here on the wall of the octagon.

"And we will grant your wish—and offer you,
    if you should change your mind, the option to
    decline.
For you are ample evidence that poets have more sea
    within them
    than fear, and that's a danger:
Great courage is like big money: you can build great
    things with it
    but destroy them too, whatever your design."

PART 13

As if coming out of a dream, I find myself back at
    the three-way gorge
    All three now are marked as "exit." Right or
    wrong?

---

28. Prasthanatrayi: the hoped-for complete collection of the Upanishads, including the lost books. See also p. 203n21.

Exit from what? From myself? From the murk and
>steam of the place?
>>or from the ocean world itself?
Another bubble bursts. I read the lightning written
>there,
>>the first text yet in my Albanian tongue.

"Dear blood kin, one last message. Blessings and
>good luck,
>>and think before you act. Take this with you:
India is a horizon of all human civilization:
>the closer you get, the further it is away.
>Farewell."
I'm troubled by these words from Mother Teresa:
>I've lost my counselors, the book, and now her
>too.

I took the left fork; now I don't know why
>the heart side seemed the way to follow;
I'm free to move to either side or down,
>but overhead a reddish veil now hems me in,
And from this strange outlandish sky
>tears of honey brown now billow.

I seek to merge my mind with the Lord Shiva
>to know where I should go and where I am, but
>all in vain.
I feel an angst, as in the ditch of the devil
>scorpions—
>>but this time I am in control.

Insomniac, undreaming, weighed down like the cripples
    who beg upon Calcutta's streets, I bear the pain.

Upon my left I see what seems a building in construction,
    an empty architecture strange and rare,
Enlarging as I near it, rising from a bed
    of pink and white and yellow pearls:
It is a giant whale, a skeleton, and in its jaws
    another fish, bones also, hiding there.

The outer skeleton is so heaped up
    with pearls their light's dim shine
Seems almost to restore the flesh of that within,
    a jawfish by its looks,
But peaked along its spine
    as if an ancient pyramid or shrine.

"Stop! This was a tragedy, from thirty million years ago,
    and we do not permit a closer view."
A saw shark is hovering above the sand,
    its two-edged saw now threatening my knees.
But I crane forward, and an electric eel
    darts in before my eyes and shocks me through and through.

When I recovered knew that I had been unconscious
    and I was deep within the danger zone.

That fish had not died by its act of loving incubation,
>   taking the female's poured-out eggs into his mouth.
Within the jaws were three gold eggs, huge as an ostrich's,
>   Containing something surely crying to be known.

I burst out then: "I beg you, one great egg be studied by the scholars,
>   for humankind must know what they make known."
Hundreds of fish had gathered, caged me in: it seemed
>   I should say something vital, more than life itself.
I stammered on: "We must, for those eggs are for us
>   as gold in gold, and bone within the bone."

At once they shed the cubic cage about me,
>   and formed a hovering plus or cross before the eggs.
Like them, I made a cross and said I knew a fact,
>   and with it an idea that might be now of value.
"What can you offer that we do not know?" the sawfish said,
>   but drew her sword back from between my legs.

I said: "The lost 257 Upanishads are found;
>   so the 365 Prasthanatrayi are complete.

That is the fact. The thought: the poets and
    philosophers
        of all the creeds and tongues shall write a sacred
        scripture for the sea."
And now I gave a eulogy for all the fish,
    placing my hand there where my hot heart beat.

"Often I've flung my arms out in despair,
    following you all from advent to cessation,
Seeing you teach your newborns how to swim
    unfearing
        that they must share the sun and sea with
        humankind,
Unknowing that their lovely grace of motion and
    their charm
        might for our children, too, be revelation.

"You overlooked the reason why their young
    should fear not only other fish but humans too,
Granted their easy innocence about the threats we
    posed
        against their peaceful ways,
Opened the path of life to them, believing
    That God created all and loved whatever grew.

"I have seen fishermen cast out their nets
    like batwings, so betraying you;
Saw others tossing dynamite with detonators
    set to kill you in your homes;

Have seen them use your hunger to undo you,
    bait dying on the hook that kills you too.

"I, the poet who calls out these words,
    have seen your young shudder before they died,
Wince while their scales are flayed and flesh is sliced,
    in their last effort so to please us,
Just to be baked or boiled or fried and eaten
    without remorse—for pleasure not for hungry
    need.

"But who will notice their wide eyes that cannot
    close
    throughout this horrifying hour,
The eaters' jaws open and close again,
    but the fish's mouth gapes ever in amazement;
More than ever do I feel the guilt of thinking it
    enough
    that I have never eaten fish when it was in my
    power.

"Though it's too late to ask for your forgiveness,
    for many have already lost both life and breath,
I still ask pardon for the portion of my guilt
    for the pollution of your waters;
With unclean oil and greenhouse gas we sucked
    your life out with your oxygen and left you death.

"I bless the fish, for fish are poets, both alike in faith
    that even if they die, they die in beauty then;

For fish and poets not poverty nor terror, nor yet death
 can shut their eyes and mouths.
So now with anguished heart I spread my arms to make
 for you parentheses of care. Amen."

PART 14

Reflected in the eye of the blue whale that has joined me
 I can see myself, a golden egg within my hands;
Vishnu has sensed the crisis of my mission
 and seeks now to balance out its evil and its good.
He's shaped and sent for me a ray of energy, tuned in infrared
 but brushed with ultraviolet bands,

Projecting sharply on a cliff of magnetite
 the amber image of an X, a cross,
But closer up I see that it denotes
 the chromosomes of Vikram Sarabhai the astrophysicist,
Whose center is a sketch of two hands clasped in prayer
 directed to the south, the lands of loss.

I take from this that I must think not as a poet,
 but as a scientist—there is a world to save.

I pass through a mosaic of unknown minerals
   that shine like mirrors, dizzying,
Until I reach a great crag south of the blue Bay of
   Bengal
   and under it a crystal cave.

Two seahorses appear, and greet me:
   "Welcome to the most advanced laboratory of
   the sea.
Here life and death experiment with one another;
   here you will find the divine codes of the soul of
   India,
The genome of your poetics, the formula that will
   restructure
   the neurons of your brain and set you free.

"The egg you hold is one of three that hold
   engraved in art and gold the moral codes of
   India,
It is the last of the three million years
   of communal wisdom written here in whale
   song,
Set in a nest of a billion sheets of mica
   and stored in the sacred fish's jaw.

"Within that greater maw, the whale's, that found
   this place to die
   is saved the human traces that survived the test
   of time.

You're the least likely man in all the world to bear
 this mission,
 but then perhaps that why you're here.
It is a signal privilege for you to see the solar energy
 unfold those codes in symbol and in rhyme.

"'Vishnu has held back a part of solar energy
 to shine for you.' But there's one last thing you
 must learn:
The egg stays here, for it's not yet decided
 if humankind is ready for it.
Explicit knowledge now would mar your pilgrimage
 to Saint Teresa,
 lost there, forever an outsider, and with no
 return.

"Fast before you enter, swear by the sea poets'
 testament
 to keep our secret secret, lock its door.
All you learn here, to serve humanity, must be
 confined
 in the hermetic metaphors of poetry."
I bent until my heart could touch the testament
 bound in its rough fish scales, and swore.

Gjekë Marinaj is an Albanian-born American poet, writer, world literature scholar and translator, and literary critic. He earned a PhD in humanities at the University of Texas at Dallas.

The founder of Protonism Theory, a form of arts criticism that aims to promote peace and positive thinking, Marinaj has published more than twenty-five books of poetry, journalism, criticism, and translation. His works have been translated and published in more than two dozen languages.

In addition to holding the title of Nation's Ambassador, Albania's highest cultural honor, he has received South Korea's Suwon KS and Changwon KC International Literary Prizes, Uzbekistan's Poet of the World Prize, and India's World Poet Prize. He has received multiple nominations for the Nobel Prize in Literature.

Marinaj is the director of Mundus Artium Press and co-editor of *Mundus Artium: A Journal of International Literature and the Arts*. As a professor, he oversees doctoral dissertations for multiple universities worldwide.

Frederick Turner is Founders Professor of Arts and Humanities (emeritus) at the University of Texas at Dallas, and was educated at Oxford University. A poet, critic, translator, philosopher, and former editor of the *Kenyon Review*, he has authored over forty books, most recently *Latter Days* (Colosseum Books, 2022). With Zsuzsanna Ozsváth he has published several volumes of Hungarian and German poetry in translation.

His work has been contributed the fields of literary and critical theory, Shakespeare studies, the biological foundation of poetic meter, restoration ecology, epic studies, the history and philosophy of science and technology, translation theory, artificial intelligence, time, and poetics. He has been nominated over forty times for the Nobel Prize for Literature and translated into over a dozen languages.

www.ingramcontent.com/pod-product-compliance
Lightning Source LLC
Chambersburg PA
CBHW030059291125
36065CB00027B/1177